Teaching
RED SCARF GIRL

Created to Accompany the Memoir *Red Scarf Girl*, by Ji-li Jiang

FACING
HISTORY
AND
OURSELVES

Facing History and Ourselves is an international educational and professional development organization whose mission is to engage students of diverse backgrounds in an examination of racism, prejudice, and antisemitism in order to promote the development of a more humane and informed citizenry. By studying the historical development of the Holocaust and other examples of genocide, students make the essential connection between history and the moral choices they confront in their own lives. For more information about Facing History and Ourselves, please visit our website at *www.facinghistory.org*.

The front cover illustration is a section from a propaganda poster created during the beginning of the Cultural Revolution (1966–1968), the same years Ji-li describes in her memoir. Since the founding of the People's Republic of China 1949, government and party officials used mass-produced posters as a way to promote nationalism and convey the values of the Communist Party. Propaganda posters were especially important during the Cultural Revolution, and this poster represents many dominant themes of this media: the glorification of Mao, the color red symbolizing China and the Chinese Communist Party, and the depiction of youth as foot-soldiers for the revolution. The slogan on the poster expresses a popular anthem of the era: Chairman Mao is the Reddest Reddest Red Sun in Our Hearts. For more teaching materials on propaganda posters in this study guide, refer to *Part 3: Obedience to the Revolution*.

Cover art photo: *Crowd of Red Guards* courtesy of University of Westminster Chinese Poster Collection, London; *Red Scarf Girl* cover jacket courtesy of HarperCollins Publishers.

To order classroom copies, please fax a purchase order to 617-232-0281 or call 617-232-1595 to place a phone order.

To download a PDF of this guide free of charge, please visit *www.facinghistory.org/redscarfgirl*.

 FACING HISTORY AND OURSELVES

Headquarters
16 Hurd Road
Brookline, MA 02445
(617) 232-1595
www.facinghistory.org

ABOUT FACING HISTORY AND OURSELVES

Facing History and Ourselves is a nonprofit educational organization whose mission is to engage students of diverse backgrounds in an examination of racism, prejudice, and antisemitism in order to promote a more humane and informed citizenry. As the name Facing History and Ourselves implies, the organization helps teachers and their students make the essential connections between history and the moral choices they confront in their own lives, and it offers a framework and a vocabulary for analyzing the meaning and responsibility of citizenship and the tools to recognize bigotry and indifference in their own worlds. Through a rigorous examination of the failure of democracy in Germany during the 1920s and '30s and the steps leading to the Holocaust, along with other examples of hatred, collective violence, and genocide in the past century, Facing History and Ourselves provides educators with tools for teaching history and ethics, and for helping their students learn to combat prejudice with compassion, indifference with participation, myth and misinformation with knowledge.

Believing that no classroom exists in isolation, Facing History and Ourselves offers programs and materials to a broad audience of students, parents, teachers, civic leaders, and all of those who play a role in the education of young people. Through significant higher-education partnerships, Facing History and Ourselves also reaches and impacts teachers before they enter their classrooms.

By studying the choices that led to critical episodes in history, students learn how issues of identity and membership, ethics and judgment have meaning today and in the future. Facing History and Ourselves' resource books provide a meticulously researched yet flexible structure for examining complex events and ideas. Educators can select appropriate readings and draw on additional resources available online or from our comprehensive lending library.

Our foundational resource book, *Facing History and Ourselves: Holocaust and Human Behavior*, embodies a sequence of study that begins with identity—first individual identity and then group and national identities, with their definitions of membership. From there the program examines the failure of democracy in Germany and the steps leading to the Holocaust—the most documented case of twentieth-century indifference, de-humanization, hatred, racism, antisemitism, and mass murder. It goes on to explore difficult questions of judgment, memory, and legacy, and the necessity for responsible participation to prevent injustice. *Facing History and Ourselves* then returns to the theme of civic participation to examine stories of individuals, groups, and nations who have worked to build just and inclusive communities and whose stories illuminate the courage, compassion, and political will that are needed to protect democracy today and in generations to come. Other examples in which civic dilemmas test democracy, such as the Armenian Genocide and the U.S. civil rights movement, expand and deepen the connection between history and the choices we face today and in the future.

Facing History and Ourselves has offices or resource centers in the United States, Canada, and the United Kingdom, as well as in-depth partnerships in Rwanda, South Africa, and Northern Ireland. Facing History and Ourselves' outreach is global, with educators trained in more than 80 countries and delivery of our resources through a website accessed worldwide with online content delivery, a program for international fellows, and a set of NGO partnerships. By convening conferences of scholars, theologians, educators, and journalists, Facing History and Ourselves' materials are kept timely, relevant, and responsive to salient issues of global citizenship in the twenty-first century.

For more than 30 years, Facing History and Ourselves has challenged students and educators to connect the complexities of the past to the moral and ethical issues of today. They explore democratic values and consider what it means to exercise one's rights and responsibilities in the service of a more humane and compassionate world. They become aware that "little things are big"—seemingly minor decisions can have a major impact and change the course of history.

For more about Facing History and Ourselves, visit our website at *www.facinghistory.org.*

ACKNOWLEDGMENTS

Primary writer: Elisabeth Fieldstone Kanner

We greatly appreciate Anla Cheng and Mark Kingdon for their generous support of *Teaching* Red Scarf Girl. William A. Joseph, Professor of Political Science at Wellesley College, contributed to the historical rigor of this guide through his meticulously written introduction and his thoughtful review of the manuscript. We appreciate the support of Ji-li Jiang for telling us her story and allowing us to bring it into the classroom.

We also value the efforts of our own staff in producing and implementing the guide. Margot Stern Strom shepherded this project from its inception. We are especially grateful to our core editorial team on this project: Marc Skvirsky, Adam Strom, Dimitry Anselme, Denise Gelb, Jimmie Jones, and Elisabeth Fieldstone Kanner. Alana McDonough and Chelsea Prosser helped bring this guide to completion.

Developing this unit required the efforts of individuals throughout the organization. We would like to call special attention to the following members of the Facing History community for their assistance with this project: Catherine O'Keefe, Maria Hill, Rachel Murray, Bonnie Oberman, and Pam Haas. We thank, too, Sharon Lindenburger, for copyediting the text, and Brown Publishing Network for the design and production work entailed in this guide. ✪

TABLE OF CONTENTS

RATIONALE

By Adam Strom, Director of Research and Development, Facing History and Ourselves

Ji-li Jiang's extraordinary memoir *Red Scarf Girl* transports readers to a tumultuous time in Chinese history—the first two years of the Great Proletarian Cultural Revolution. Caught between conflicting forces—joining the Revolution's call for rebellion, protecting her family, and fitting in with her peers—Jiang describes how her once-"perfect" world begins to crumble. What might young people all over the world learn from reading Jiang's story about growing up during this period?

Though this guide aims to help teachers and students explore *Red Scarf Girl* in its particular historical context, Facing History and Ourselves is rooted in a pedagogy that identifies concerns and choices adolescents confront each day and uses them as connections for students to move back and forth between understanding choices of the past and the present—the bridge between history and ourselves. Students learn to recognize distinctions among events, to draw appropriate connections, and to grasp similar issues without making facile comparisons and imperfect parallels. Through deep examination of particular case studies, students gain an awareness of universal themes of prejudice and discrimination, as well as courage, caring, and responsible participation. The teaching activities in this guide encourage this kind of reflection.

In her memoir, Jiang struggles with questions about her identity and loyalty and the conflicting forces of authority, conformity, and obedience. These dilemmas are familiar to many adolescents, who navigate these challenges in their own lives. Our 32 years of experience have taught us that students are best able to learn and understand history by searching for connections between the events they are studying and their own personal experiences. Therefore, Facing History resources are rooted in the major concerns and issues of adolescence: in the overarching interest in individual and group identity; in acceptance or rejection, in conformity or non-conformity, in labeling, ostracism, loyalty, fairness, and peer-group pressure. What makes *Red Scarf Girl* such a compelling read for adolescents is that Ji-li Jiang's story highlights how the Cultural Revolution heightened these dilemmas for millions of adolescents in China. By reading about how Jiang and her peers navigated through the complex ethical issues of that time, students have the opportunity to reflect on decisions they have made, and will make, about their own roles as members of families, peer groups, and a national community.

Educators in the Facing History and Ourselves network will recognize the power of *Red Scarf Girl* to engage young people as emerging moral philosophers. For those of you new to our program, we hope that you will learn more about us. Like *Red Scarf Girl*, many of our other resources address stories of youth in difficult historical moments, including children in the Hitler Youth, immigrants in contemporary Europe, and young people who participated in the United States civil rights movement. Please visit *www.facinghistory.org* to see our list of publications, download a study guide, take a workshop, or contact your nearest Facing History and Ourselves office.

HISTORICAL BACKGROUND

By William A. Joseph, Wellesley College

Over the course of two days in early August 1966, students at the prestigious Girls Middle School, which was attached to Beijing Normal University,* psychologically browbeat and physically tortured Bian Zhongyun, a teacher and vice principal, including pummeling her with wooden sticks spiked with nails. They eventually dumped her—alive—into a garbage cart. By the time someone wheeled the cart to a nearby hospital, Bian was dead. She was 50 years old at the time of her murder and had worked at the school for 17 years. Her husband received a call from the hospital and, with their four children, went to identify her body. There was no investigation because, in essence, Bian Zhongyun was judged to have gotten what she deserved.

How could this happen? Why would a group of high school students beat one of their teachers to death? Why would many other students (and some teachers) stand around and watch it happen? And why would those who did it not be arrested and punished—in fact, why would they be praised as heroes and leaders? Bian Zhongyun was just the first of many teachers to be beaten to death—or driven to suicide—by high school students in Beijing, and elsewhere in China, during what has come to be known as "Red August" in the early days of the Great Proletarian Cultural Revolution in China. This political movement, launched in May 1966 by Chairman Mao Zedong, the head of the Chinese Communist Party (CCP), was aimed at ridding the country of those he had concluded were betraying his goals to create a communist society.

By the mid-1960s, Chairman Mao had become vey unhappy about the way China was developing. The educational system was rigid and extremely competitive, with just a very small percentage of students being able to go to the best schools or get into a college of any kind. There were hierarchies within the industrial working class, between those with secure jobs and generous benefits in state-owned enterprises, and growing ranks of contract workers with no such security or benefits.[1]

There was also the nearly iron wall between urban and rural China, put in place in the mid-1950s under the "household registration system" (the *hukou* system) that consigned each citizen to live and work in either the cities or the countryside, with no chance of geographic or job mobility. There was repression and pent-up frustration of various kinds in China on the eve of the Cultural Revolution. Almost non-stop political campaigns against alleged enemies of the Communist Party since the early 1950s left many people, even those not targeted, tense and hypersensitive about what might be coming next. In sum, Chinese society was in many ways ready to explode, and Chairman Mao's call for a Cultural Revolution to set China in a new direction was the spark that ignited it.[2]

Students at schools throughout China were both excited and incited by the start of the Cultural Revolution. They formed organizations called "Red Guards" that pledged allegiance to Chairman Mao, whom they had been brought up to see as the infallible

---

*In China, middle school is the equivalent of high school in the United States, coming between elementary school and university, and encompassing students ages 14–19. A "normal university" is a university that specializes in training teachers for elementary and high schools.

savior of their nation. Teachers and school administrators like Bian Zhongyun were among the first targets of the Cultural Revolution.[3] They were accused of having committed serious ideological mistakes, such as looking down on working people, transmitting politically incorrect ideas to students, favoring foreign books or art, and leading easy and decadent lives. The Red Guards were only too eager to take the lead in identifying and isolating these alleged counterrevolutionaries in their midst. As adult authority melted away out of fear, and the police and army were ordered to stay on the sidelines and let the movement take its course, the young rebels used their power in increasingly brutal ways—first against the "enemies" of Chairman Mao, and then in violent clashes with each other as they broke into factions, each claiming the purest fidelity to the Chairman and the ideals of the Cultural Revolution.

It is also important to take note of the violence of the language of the Cultural Revolution, and of Chinese politics in general, during the era when Mao Zedong was in power (1949–1976). Ever since the founding of the People's Republic of China (PRC) in 1949, the Communist Party had created a sharp, if constantly changing, dividing line between the "people" who supported the CCP and their "enemies" who wanted to dethrone the party and return China to the evil days of elitism and exploitation. From the early 1950s on, these "class enemies" were tagged with a variety of labels: counterrevolutionaries, rightists, revisionists, spies, and traitors, to name a few. This, by definition, already made them "non-people," but they also came to be called "poisonous weeds," "cow monsters and snake demons," "ox ghosts," "running dogs," "vampires," and other epithets that literally dehumanized them. In the Cultural Revolution, the enemies of the people were to be "knocked down," "dragged out," "unmasked," "struggled against," "swept away," "smashed," confined to makeshift jail cells called "cowsheds," and paraded in the streets wearing dunce caps and signboards depicting them as criminals deserving execution. In the ideologically charged context of the times, it was not a big step from violent, dehumanizing language and demeaning gestures to torture and murder.

WHAT WAS THE GREAT PROLETARIAN CULTURAL REVOLUTION?[4]

The origins of the Cultural Revolution can be traced back to the mid-1950s when the leadership of the Chinese Communist Party (CCP) began to show ideological and political cracks that would widen greatly over the next decade.[5] These leaders had been generally unified in their approach to governing China under the leadership of Chairman Mao Zedong since coming to power in 1949. But within a few years of the founding of the PRC, differences among them emerged over issues such as the speed and scope of the collectivization of agriculture. Mao Zedong generally favored a faster pace of collectivization and of other aspects of China's socialist construction, while some of his colleagues at the top preferred a more gradual transition. Given Mao's absolute power, he always got his way.

Mao's way led in early 1958 to the launching of the Great Leap Forward, a radical, utopian effort both to accelerate China's development in order to catch up economically with the West, and to achieve a truly egalitarian communist society in a short span of time. The engine of economic and ideological change was to be the labor, will power, and revolutionary enthusiasm of the masses under the guidance of party leaders, from Chairman Mao at the top to those in the million or so villages of rural China.[6]

The crack in the party leadership widened significantly in August 1959, when Mao rejected the advice of China's defense minister and one of the CCP's most senior officials, Peng Dehuai, to adjust the radical policies of the Great Leap because signs of famine were beginning to appear in the countryside. Mao not only did not scale back the Leap but, in fact, revved it up. He also dismissed Peng from office and denounced him for being a "right opportunist"—someone who opposes socialism and the party— steps that reflected a major escalation of the stakes involved in the CCP's elite politics.

The Great Leap Forward ended in disaster in 1961. The worst famine in human history took the lives of 20–30 million Chinese peasants. An industrial depression wiped out many of the economic gains made during the CCP's first decade in power. The causes of the tragedy were many, including a long stretch of very bad weather in many parts of the country. But the responsibility for the catastrophe must ultimately fall on Mao for initiating the Leap and for insisting on continuing it even in the face of mounting problems and impending catastrophe.

The famine left deep scars in the Chinese countryside; yet rural people, knowing nothing of the national scale of suffering, tended to blame local leaders, although very few of them were ever held accountable. Those in the urban areas were told the Leap failed because of natural disasters and the treachery of the Soviet Union. The Soviets had pulled all of their advisors out of China and cut off all aid in 1960 because of increasing tensions between Moscow and Beijing on matters of both foreign and domestic policy. The Soviets favored "peaceful coexistence" with the United States, while Chairman Mao preferred confrontation and promoting revolutionary movements in the Third World. The emergence of this "Sino-Soviet" split in the late 1950s and early 1960s would have profound consequences on Mao's thinking, and on his perception of trends in Chinese politics and society, which would ultimately lead him to embark on the Cultural Revolution.

In the aftermath of the Great Leap, the Chairman voluntarily handed over responsibility for economic policy-making to two of his most trusted comrades in the party leadership, Liu Shaoqi and Deng Xiaoping, while he himself concentrated on larger and broader matters of ideology. Liu and Deng were given the tasks of cleaning up the economic mess left by the Leap and steering the economy back toward sustained growth. Initially, they had Mao's support for their efforts, and those efforts yielded positive results fairly quickly. But during 1962–1965, the Chairman grew increasingly alarmed at the kinds of policies being pursued by Liu and Deng and at some of the consequences for Chinese society.

In industry, the recovery policies emphasized managerial authority, technical knowledge, and worker discipline. In agriculture, peasants were allowed great leeway in deciding what to plant and how to farm the land, without having to take orders from above. The spirit of the policy in the rural areas was captured in the now famous remark made by Deng Xiaoping in a speech at a conference on agriculture production in 1962: "It doesn't matter if a cat is black or white, as long as it catches mice."[7] In other words, the success of an economic policy should be measured by whether it increases production, not by some abstract yardstick of ideological correctness. In general, the expertise of intellectuals and scientists was lauded for its importance in China's modernization, without reference to the previous formula that they had to be both "red and expert" to be considered politically reliable. Even in the arts, there was greater freedom of creation and expression.

However, Mao saw such policies as the source of elitism, bureaucratization, inequality, corruption, and ideological degeneration both within the CCP and Chinese society at large. He began to scold his colleagues with comments such as, "The Ministry of Public Health is not a Ministry of Public Health for the people, so why not change its name to the Ministry of Urban Health, the Ministry of Gentlemen's Health, or even the Ministry of Urban Gentlemen's Health? . . . In medical and health work, put the emphasis on the countryside!"[8] His displeasure extended to the realm of education, which he declared "ruins talent and ruins youth. I do not approve of reading so many books. The method of examination is a method for dealing with the enemy; it is most harmful, and should be stopped. . . . We must put into practice the union of education and productive labor."[9] Actors, poets, and writers, he exclaimed, should be driven "out of the cities, and pack[ed] . . . off to the countryside. They should all periodically go down in batches to the villages and to the factories. We must not let writers stay in the government offices; they will never get anything written if they do not go down. Whoever does not go down will get no dinner; only when they go down will they be fed."[10]

Most ominously, Mao often warned that there was not enough attention paid in the party and the country to "class struggle," and that there were still many counter-revolutionaries who wanted to overthrow the Communist Party and abandon socialism altogether. "We must acknowledge that classes will continue to exist for a long time," he noted in 1962. "We must also acknowledge the existence of a struggle of class against class, and admit the possibility of the restoration of reactionary classes."[11]

Mao's disquiet about China's direction in the early 1960s was reinforced by his conclusion that the Communist Party of the Soviet Union had become "revisionist," that is, it had betrayed and abandoned Marxism-Leninism under the leadership of Nikita Khrushchev. Furthermore, Mao determined that a form of capitalism had been restored in the Soviet Union in which the party itself was the new ruling class—a "new bourgeoisie"—exploiting the masses. In the Chairman's view, the People's Republic of China would suffer a similar fate unless some very drastic action was taken to change the country's course.

That drastic action turned out to be the Great Proletarian Cultural Revolution. It officially exploded on May 16, 1966, with the publication of a circular from the party's Central Committee that affirmed the movement as "initiated and led personally by Comrade Mao Zedong," and specifically denounced "persons like Khrushchev [who] are still trusted by us and are being trained as our successors, persons . . . who are still nestling beside us." The directive called on the revolutionary masses to launch a "life-and-death struggle" against "[t]hose representatives of the bourgeoisie who have sneaked into the party, the government, the army, and various cultural circles [and who] are a bunch of counterrevolutionary revisionists" who were plotting to seize power.[12] It was from this point that China was plunged into what is now officially referred to in the PRC as "ten years of chaos"—the Cultural Revolution, which is said to have ended only after Mao's death in 1976.[13]

Mao's primary objective was first and foremost an ideological struggle to get China off the "capitalist road" and back on the road to socialism and communism. In order to achieve this, Chinese society first had to be purified: alleged counterrevolutionaries had to be displaced from positions of power, and their corrosive influence eradicated in all aspects of life. Then a new, truly revolutionary order—a "great proletarian culture" could be built.

A second objective involved a power struggle. Mao thought that he was being ignored by Liu Shaoqi, Deng Xiaoping, and others and that his wishes were, at best, being given only lip service and, at worst, being deliberately flaunted. If he was to achieve the ideological goals of the Cultural Revolution, he would have to restore his personal power and prestige within the Communist Party.

A third objective was related to the first two: the issue of succession. Who would succeed Mao (who was over 70 in the mid-1960s) as the leader of the CCP and ensure that his vision for a revolutionary China would live on? But beyond the matter of *personal* succession was a larger question, that of *generational* succession. If the young people of China had been corrupted and seduced by the bourgeois ideology that was poisoning the educational system and culture, then there was no hope for the future of his revolution.[14] Therefore, one goal of the movement was to "train and bring up millions of successors who will carry on the cause of proletarian revolution" by testing and tempering the youth in "mass struggles" and the "great storms of revolution."[15]

THE STAGES OF THE CULTURAL REVOLUTION

The Cultural Revolution was such a complicated event, which unfolded in a series of tumultuous twists and turns, that it almost defies chronological telling.[16] One approach to understanding the movement is to dissect it into three distinct stages: Stage I: Mobilization and Chaos, 1966–1969; Stage II: Order and Horror, 1969–1971; Stage III: The Succession Showdown, 1972–1976. It is important to point out that this approach gives the appearance of much more orderly planning than was the case with the Cultural Revolution. Much of what happened was unplanned and unforeseen by Mao or anyone else.

STAGE I: MOBILIZATION AND CHAOS, 1966–1969

This was the most destructive stage of the Cultural Revolution. Indeed, destruction was its major purpose. The May 16 Circular cited approvingly Chairman Mao's earlier declaration that "there is no construction without destruction," and went on to instruct its audience to "Put destruction first, and in the process you have construction."[17] Such instructions gave authority to the Red Guard campaign to destroy the "four olds"—old customs, culture, habits, and ideas—that led to the burning of books, the smashing of historical artifacts, the harassment of people because of decadent clothing or hairstyle, and countless forms of purification that paved the way to the beatings and torture of class enemies. The full human toll of this period of the Cultural Revolution is not known, but it is widely believed to have exceeded 1 million people killed or driven to suicide.

During this first stage of the Cultural Revolution, Mao put together a potent political coalition that would allow him to take on and overcome some of the most powerful leaders and institutions in the PRC. That coalition included the Red Guards, which as noted above, sprang up spontaneously in middle schools and universities in the spring of 1966 following the CCP Central Committee's call to "follow Comrade Mao Zedong's instructions . . . thoroughly expose the reactionary bourgeois stand of those so-called 'academic authorities' who oppose the party and socialism, thoroughly criticize and repudiate the reactionary bourgeois ideas in the sphere of academic work, education, journalism, literature and art, and publishing, and seize the leadership in these cultural spheres."[18] It was in this context that Red Guards in Beijing, and elsewhere, carried out the brutalization of teachers and administrators.

In August 1966, millions of Red Guards made their way to Beijing to be greeted and blessed by Chairman Mao at a series of rallies in Tiananmen ("Gate of Heavenly Peace") Square, a huge public space at the front entrance of the Forbidden City, the one-time palace of Chinese emperors. At one rally, the Chairman donned a Red Guard armband given to him by a young rebel named Song Binbin and told her that she should change her given name from "Binbin," which means "gentle and refined" to "Yaowu," meaning "Be Militant."[19] From these rallies, the Red Guards returned to their homes and schools throughout the country to become the main foot soldiers in carrying out Mao's Cultural Revolution. They were joined by rebel groups who seized power in factories, offices, and other workplaces as the movement engulfed institutions in all parts of society.

Two other key elements in the Maoist coalition that made the Cultural Revolution possible were the army and a core group of radicals who had been relatively minor figures in the party leadership prior to the mid-1960s. The People's Liberation Army (PLA), as all of the PRC's armed forces were called, was headed at the time by Lin Biao, one of China's most famous generals. He was a fanatical Maoist who had taken charge of the military after the ouster of Peng Dehuai during the Great Leap Forward. Under Lin's command, the PLA had become a model of political virtue in stressing the importance of Mao's theories, known officially as Mao Zedong Thought, in its military training and preparation for war. It was Lin Biao who, in 1964, first authorized the publication of the *Little Red Book* of quotations from Chairman Mao in a size and format suitable for use by troops on the move. The Red Guards adopted the *Little Red Book* as their "bible" for making revolution, and also chose to wear army-style green uniforms and caps as a sign of both their admiration of the PLA and their militancy. Most importantly, Lin and the PLA high command made sure that the military supported Mao's Cultural Revolution not only rhetorically but also by staying on the sidelines while the Red Guards and other rebels ran violently amok for nearly two years.

The third pillar of Mao's Cultural Revolution coalition consisted of radical activists led by Jiang Qing, the Chairman's wife. She had been put in charge of combating reactionary trends in the arts in the early 1960s. Mao promoted Jiang, and other ideologically reliable political figures, to key positions at the center of power of this new movement. Their influence was most visible in the media and propaganda that played such an important role in creating the highly charged political atmosphere of the Cultural Revolution. The radicals replaced the purged senior leaders, including Liu Shaoqi, who died in 1969 from brutal maltreatment, and Deng Xiaoping, who was sent to work in a rural factory.

In 1967 and 1968, armed clashes broke out among Red Guard factions and other groups over which one was most faithful to Chairman Mao, or which one would hold the upper hand politically within their institutions. At this point, Mao sent the army to stop the violence (which they often did by using violence) to restore order, and then dispatched as many as 20 million urban Red Guards "up to the mountains and down to the countryside" to work alongside and be re-educated by the peasants. The intervention of the military, the demobilization of the Red Guards, and the restoration of institutional political authority marked the end of the first stage of the Cultural Revolution and the beginning of the second.

STAGE II: ORDER AND HORROR, 1968–1971

Between the years 1968–1971, the People's Liberation Army held an unprecedented position of political power in the PRC. At the top, Lin Biao was officially designated as Mao's successor, and there was a large increase in the number of military personnel leading party and state organizations. The military also took the lead in establishing "revolutionary committees," which were the new form of administration set up to run cities, provinces, and other levels of government, as well as institutions such as universities and factories. Besides representatives from the PLA, the revolutionary committees were to be made up of experienced officials who had been judged politically reliable and "mass representatives" chosen from Red Guard or other rebel groups.

Order was restored, and the large-scale public violence of the Red Guards ended. Yet this involved a more orderly kind of violence: a "cleansing of class ranks" campaign. This began with Mao's authorization in 1968, intensified in early 1969, and was guided most often by the PLA-led revolutionary committees. Special "Mao Zedong Thought Propaganda Teams" were deployed to various workplaces to carry out "examinations" of people accused of counter-revolutionary ideas, actions, or connections, whether in the present or remote past. Teachers and other intellectuals were again prime targets,[20] but the campaign also often provided an opportunity for those now in power to exact revenge against their previous factional opponents. Furthermore, "cleansing the class ranks" extended the violence of the Cultural Revolution deeper into the countryside, where, for example, former landlords and their families—long deprived of their land and wealth, and sometimes even moved to the city—were hauled back to their native villages to be "struggled" against and, in many cases, persecuted to death.[21] In more than a few cases, Mao's loyalists were so eager to thoroughly eradicate the alleged "renegades, scabs, and traitors" that they literally devoured them in acts of politically motivated cannibalism.[22] This campaign, and a similarly vicious one in 1970–71, added another 1–2 million lives to the toll of the Cultural Revolution, with many millions more suffering serious physical and psychological injuries.

The pivotal event of this period was the appearance of another crack in the top leadership of the CCP, this time between Chairman Mao and his designated "close comrade-in-arms and successor," Lin Biao. The "Lin Biao Affair" is one of the most bizarre episodes of this period. It appears that by 1970, Mao had come to believe that the PLA had too much political power and that it had been a mistake to put Lin in a position to succeed him as chairman of the CCP. Having already detached himself from one part of his Cultural Revolution coalition, the Red Guards, and other mass rebel organizations, Mao now decided he no longer needed the military to maintain his personal power.

Through various decisions and remarks, Mao clearly showed that he was unhappy with Lin and favored Jiang Qing and her fellow radicals within the top decision-making bodies. Lin Biao's politically influential wife, Ye Qun, and their son, Lin Liguo, a high-ranking PLA air force officer, began secret discussions about carrying out a coup d'état, and even about assassinating Mao. But their plot was foiled, and, in panic, on September 12, 1971, together with Lin Biao, they attempted to flee by plane to the Soviet Union. The plane crashed in Mongolia, killing all aboard.

Although the official CCP story is that Lin Biao was at the center of the plot to seize power, his personal involvement in the coup plans is unclear. He was in poor health and not known for being particularly decisive or proactive in political matters. The weight of scholarly opinion is that he was relatively passive when the showdown came, compared to other members of his family. In any case, Mao got what he wanted out of Lin's demise and the subsequent arrest of the most powerful members of his military faction in the leadership: the return of the PLA to the barracks and its withdrawal from the political battlefront.

STAGE III: THE SUCCESSION SHOWDOWN, 1972–1976

The last stage of the Cultural Revolution was much less violent than the previous two but was more fateful in determining China's future. It set the stage and cleared the way for the country's move away from Maoist priorities and policies after the Chairman's death in 1976, which in turn made possible the country's breathtaking economic growth in recent decades.

The central dynamic of this period was a political tug-of-war between Jiang Qing's radical faction and a more moderate faction of leaders headed initially by Zhou Enlai, the premier (or prime minister) of China since 1949. Zhou Enlai had survived the Cultural Revolution by following Mao's instructions and not challenging the Chairman's will or whims. The radicals wanted to continue the main thrust of the Cultural Revolution in terms of emphasizing ideological purity and political vigilance against class enemies. The moderates wanted the country to shift its priority to economic development and to reduce the political intensity of the Cultural Revolution. The moderate forces were bolstered by the political re-emergence in 1973 of Deng Xiaoping, who was allowed by Mao to resume his high-level positions after writing a self-criticism in which he admitted making ideological mistakes.

Throughout this tug-of-war between the radicals and moderates, Mao was very much in command, at least until near the end of his life in September 1976. He presided over the rebuilding of party and state institutions, the rehabilitation of officials, like Deng, who had been ousted during the Cultural Revolution but were now deemed sufficiently reformed to resume office, and the promotion of a younger generation of leaders. There were times when the Chairman clearly backed a trend toward moderation, particularly in economic matters, but also times when he took action that showed he was not willing to abandon the Cultural Revolution altogether. As a result, this period is marked by noticeable swings in both policy and rhetoric, but the instability remained mostly a struggle for power at the very top and never spilled out into society at large, except for minor economic disruption, public political rallies, and jangled nerves caused by several shrill propaganda campaigns with names like "Expose False Marxist Swindlers like Liu

Shaoqi," "Criticize Lin Biao, Criticize Confucius," and "Oppose the Right Deviationist Wind to Reverse the Correct Verdicts of the Cultural Revolution."

The final act in this decade-long drama came in several distinct scenes through much of 1976. It began on January 8 with the death of Zhou Enlai, who had been suffering from terminal cancer for some time. This posed the immediate issue of who would succeed Zhou as premier of the PRC. While Zhou was ill, Mao had put Deng Xiaoping in charge of running the government, but by late 1975, both Zhou and Deng had lost Mao's favor again because of his perception that their policies were, in effect, diluting the ideals of the Cultural Revolution. However, Mao had also shown displeasure with the political maneuverings of his wife, Jiang Qing, and her close radical followers. Since 1974, he had been warning them about their secretive factional activities and in 1975 admonished them, saying, "Unite and don't split; be open and aboveboard, and don't intrigue and conspire. Don't function as a gang of four, don't do it any more, why do you keep doing it?"[23]

To replace Zhou as premier, Mao made a surprising choice, picking the relatively young (55-year-old) and little-known Hua Guofeng, who had only recently been promoted to the central leadership and did not have a strong identification with either the moderate or radical factions. Hua, initially appointed *acting* premier, was someone Mao could trust, totally dependent on the Chairman and politically beholden to no one else.

In another surprising turn of events, in early April, hundreds of thousands of ordinary Chinese descended on Tiananmen Square in a spontaneous tribute to the late Zhou Enlai, who had a (somewhat romanticized) reputation as the "people's premier." The occasion for the gathering was the annual Spring Festival when Chinese traditionally pay their respects to deceased ancestors. But the gathering soon turned into a protest against Jiang Qing and the radicals, with some criticism even aimed at Mao. The demonstrations were quickly suppressed and the square cleared, with a few injuries and arrests but no deaths.

The main political consequence of this so-called Tiananmen Incident was that it was labeled as a counterrevolutionary incident and blamed on Deng Xiaoping, who was summarily ousted from his position, subjected to yet another round of public denunciation as an "unrepentant capitalist roader," and once again shunted off to political exile. Meanwhile, Mao's health was declining seriously. As the summer of 1976 approached, it appeared to most observers that Jiang Qing and her supporters were gaining momentum in their bid to control the succession to Chairman Mao. Hua Guofeng had been promoted to premier (no longer "acting") and given the position as first vice-chairman of the CCP and therefore Mao's preferred successor. However, he was seen as having a very weak base of power within the party, unlikely to survive long politically once the Chairman was dead.

Mao's death on September 8, 1976, left an unstable, highly volatile balance of power in the top leadership. In the short run, it was held together by Hua Guofeng, who had the Chairman's seal of approval. After a month-long period of national mourning, the facade of unity was shattered on October 6, 1976, when Hua Guofeng, acting with the support of key party and military leaders, authorized the arrest of Jiang Qing and her three closest radical associates, who were labeled the "Gang of Four." The Gang was said to have been plotting to seize power and install Jiang Qing as head of the party. A purge of the Gang's supporters in lower positions, and throughout the country, soon followed.

The downfall of the Gang of Four was initially hailed in the official Chinese press as "a great victory for the Great Proletarian Cultural Revolution and for Mao Zedong Thought."[24] A little less than a year later, Hua Guofeng proclaimed that "the smashing of the 'gang of four' marks the triumphant conclusion of our . . . Great Proletarian Cultural Revolution."[25]

At the urging of senior officials, Chairman Hua agreed in August 1977 to exonerate Deng Xiaoping and to restore him to his positions as a vice-premier of the PRC and vice-chairman of the CCP. Deng—the "comeback kid" of Chinese politics—was able to get the backing of enough other political and military leaders to gradually push Hua and his supporters to the sidelines and then remove them from power altogether. By late 1978, Deng Xiaoping had become China's paramount leader. Once he consolidated his authority, he launched China on a path of fundamental economic reforms that reversed the direction of the Cultural Revolution and much of the Maoist era. The policies pursued by Deng (who died in 1997) and his successors, Jiang Zemin and Hu Jintao, are officially referred to as "Building Socialism with Chinese Characteristics," but their two main ingredients have been a movement toward a market economy and deepening involvement in global commerce. The results have been spectacular, and China has gone a long way down the capitalist road that Mao fought so desperately to avoid.

The final irony and most important consequence of the Cultural Revolution is that in the end, it paved the way for the coming to power of many of its own victims who were committed to finding another, very un-Maoist way for China to develop. By causing such widespread destruction and suffering, the Cultural Revolution thoroughly discredited radical communism and created the ideological conditions for the economic reforms that have so greatly improved the lives of the vast majority of Chinese since these reforms began in the early 1980s.

---

[1] Lynn T. White, *Policies of Chaos: The Organizational Causes of Violence in China's Cultural Revolution* (Princeton, NJ: Princeton University Press, 1989); John Gardner and Wilt Idema, "China's Educational Revolution," in Stuart Schram (ed.), *Authority, Participation and Cultural Change in China* (London: Cambridge University Press, 1973), 57–89; and John Wilson Lewis, "Commerce Education and Political Development in Tangshan, 1956–69," in John Wilson Lewis, *The City in Communist China* (Stanford University Press, 1971), 153–182.

[2] Fei-Ling Wang, *Organizing Through Division and Exclusion: China's Hukou System* (Stanford University Press, 2005); and Emily Honig, "Maoist Mappings of Gender: Reassessing the Red Guards," in Susan Brownell and Jeffrey N. Wasserstrom, eds., *Chinese Femininities, Chinese Masculinities: A Reader* (Berkeley, CA: University of California Press, 2002), 255–268.

[3] Youqin Wang, "Student Attacks Against Teachers: The Revolution of 1966," http://www.cnd.org/CR/english/articles/violence.htm (accessed August 28, 2009).

[4] I want to acknowledge my debt in writing this section of the essay to Frederick C. Teiwes, "Mao in Power, 1949–76," in William A. Joseph, ed., *Politics in China: An Introduction* (New York: Oxford University Press, 2010); and Roderick MacFarquhar and Michael Schoenhals, *Mao's Last Revolution* (Cambridge: Belknap Press of Harvard University Press, 2006).

[5] The definitive work on this is Roderick MacFarquhar's three-volume study, *The Origins of the Cultural Revolution* (New York: Columbia University Press, 1974–1997).

---

[6] Ralph A. Thaxton, Jr., *Catastrophe and Contention in Rural China: Mao's Great Leap Forward Famine and the Origins of Righteous Resistance in Da Fo Village* (New York: Cambridge University Press, 2008).

[7] "Restore Agricultural Production," July 7, 1962, in *Selected Works of Deng Xiaoping, Volume 1 (1938–1965)*, *http://english.peopledaily.com.cn/dengxp/* (accessed August 28, 2009).

[8] Directive on Public Health, June 26, 1965, *http://www.marxists.org/reference/archive/mao/selected-works/volume-9/mswv9_41.htm* (accessed August 28, 2009).

[9] Remarks at the Spring Festival, February 13, 1964, *http://www.marxists.org/reference/archive/mao/selected-works/volume-9/mswv9_14.htm* (accessed August 28, 2009).

[10] Ibid.

[11] Speech at the Tenth Plenum of the Eighth Central Committee, September 24, 1962, *http://www.marxists.org/reference/archive/mao/selected-works/volume-8/mswv8_63.htm* (accessed August 28, 2009).

[12] Circular of the Central Committee of the Communist Party of China on the Great Proletarian Cultural Revolution, May 16, 1966, *http://www.marxists.org/subject/china/documents/cpc/cc_gpcr.htm* (accessed August 28, 2009).

[13] There is disagreement among scholars and others about how to date the Cultural Revolution. The official Chinese version speaks of the Cultural Revolution Decade of 1966–1976. Many scholars accept this periodization and point out that it was only over the course of that ten years that all the forces unleashed by the Cultural Revolution fully played out, although ultimately in a way that was much the opposite of what Mao intended. Other scholars argue that the term "Cultural Revolution" should be limited to the period 1966 to 1968, or 1969 at the latest. They see the end of the movement coming with the disbanding of the Red Guards and the restoration of order by the People's Liberation Army. What came after was related to, but analytically distinct from, the Cultural Revolution. See Jonathan Unger, "The Cultural Revolution at the Grass Roots," *The China Journal,* no. 57 (2007), 113–117.

[14] Robert Jay Lifton, *Revolutionary Immortality: Mao Tse-Tung and the Chinese Cultural Revolution* (Random House, 1968).

[15] "On Khrushchev's Phony Communism and Its Historical Lessons for the World," July 14, 1964, 72–74, by the Editorial Department of *Renmin Ribao* (People's Daily) and *Hongqi* (Red Flag), July 14, 1964, *http://www.marx2mao.com/Other/KPC64.html#c7* (accessed August 28, 2009).

[16] A superb analytical history of the Cultural Revolution is Roderick MacFarquhar and Michael Schoenhals's *Mao's Last Revolution* (Cambridge: Belknap Press of Harvard University Press, 2006).

[17] Circular of the Central Committee of the Communist Party of China on the Great Proletarian Cultural Revolution, May 16, 1966, and "On New Democracy," January 1940, *http://www.marxists.org/reference/archive/mao/selected-works/volume-2/mswv2_26.htm* (accessed August 28, 2009).

[18] Circular of the Central Committee of the Communist Party of China on the Great Proletarian Cultural Revolution, May 16, 1966.

[19] For an update on Song Binbin, who went on to receive a Ph.D. at MIT and lives in the United States, see "On Mao's 114th Birthday, Past Catches Up to Former Red Guard Leader," *New American Media*, December 21, 2007, *http://news.newamericamedia.org/news/view_article.html?article_id=be87ff6c4b1b6142feb076155e09c5ba* (accessed August 28, 2009).

[20] Youqin Wang, "The Second Wave of Violent Persecution of Teachers: the Revolution of 1968," *http://humanities.uchicago.edu/faculty/ywang/history* (accessed August 28, 2009).

[21] Jiangsui He, "The Death of a Landlord: Moral Predicament in Rural China, 1968–69," in Joseph W. Esherick, Paul G. Pickowicz, and Andrew G. Walder, editors, *The Chinese Cultural Revolution as History* (Shorenstein Asia-Pacific Research Center Series) (Stanford, California: Stanford University Press, 2006).

[22] Yi Zheng, *Scarlet Memorial: Tales of Cannibalism in Modern China* (Boulder, CO: Westview Press, 1994).

[23] Beijing Reviews archives, *http://www.bjreview.com.cn/nation/txt/2009-05/26/content_197544.htm* (accessed August 28, 2009).

[24] "A Great Historic Victory," editorial by Renmin Ribao, Hongqi and Jiefangjun Bao, translated and published in Beijing Review, No. 44, October 25, 1976, *http://www.bjreview.com.cn/nation/txt/2009-05/26/content_197544_2.htm* (accessed August 28, 2009).

[25] Political Report to Eleventh National Congress of the Communist Party of China, *Xinhua General News Service*, August 23, 1977.

USING THIS STUDY GUIDE

A Facing History and Ourselves student once said, "I faced history one day and found myself," articulating one of the main objectives of our materials. Rather than explore moral dilemmas and concepts of human behavior through hypothetical situations, Facing History selects particularly powerful moments in history that can be mined for ethical choices that are relevant to adolescents' lives and their emerging responsibilities as members of local, national, and global communities. The Cultural Revolution in China represents one of these powerful moments, and Ji-li Jiang's memoir *Red Scarf Girl* (HarperCollins Publishers, 1997) provides an insightful window into the tumultuous first two years of this event.

This study guide has been developed to help educators use the memoir *Red Scarf Girl* as a tool to help students explore the history of the Cultural Revolution and better understand conformity, obedience, responsibility, prejudice, indoctrination and belonging, and other factors that shaped the choices made by Chinese, especially many Chinese adolescents, in the 1960s. The study guide has been divided into seven parts. The first part, "Pre-reading," provides ideas about how you might introduce your students to the themes and historical context addressed in *Red Scarf Girl*. Parts 1–5 cover several chapters each (approximately 50 pages) of *Red Scarf Girl*. Part 6 focuses on the epilogue and suggests how to help students synthesize their learning about the Cultural Revolution and reflect on how issues raised in the text relate to society today. Because classroom contexts vary depending on students' interests, skill levels, and prior knowledge, we expect that teachers will adapt the ideas in this guide to meet their students' particular strengths and needs.

Each part is divided into two main sections: the **Overview** and **Suggested Activities**. The **Overview** provides information and questions that will support the use of *Red Scarf Girl* in the classroom. The **Overview** does the following:

- provides a summary of key events from the relevant chapters of *Red Scarf Girl*
- places these events in their historical context
- connects what is happening in *Red Scarf Girl* and the Cultural Revolution to themes that are rooted in the concerns and issues of adolescence

We believe this background information is helpful because students are more engaged—and, therefore, typically learn material more effectively—when the topics they study are connected to their own lives. We also encourage all teachers to read the Historical Background to this study guide, written by China scholar William A. Joseph, for a deeper overview and analysis of the Cultural Revolution and its legacy.

The **Overview** also contains several essential questions that can be used to guide classroom discussions and assessments. These questions frame issues and events that emerge in *Red Scarf Girl* in terms of universal aspects of human behavior. Students can use these essential questions to analyze *Red Scarf Girl* and to reflect upon their own beliefs, experiences, and understanding of today's society. In this way, essential questions help students build bridges between the text and their own lives. You will notice that many of the questions included in the Discussions and Journal Writing section are versions of the essential questions that have been applied to specific events in *Red Scarf Girl*.

The **Suggested Activities** section is divided into three parts, each of which is described below:

- **Discussions and Journal Writing:** Students learn best in conversation with themselves and others. Therefore, Facing History encourages teachers to use journals and discussions as primary teaching strategies. Writing in a journal often helps students process ideas and formulate questions; journal writing helps students prepare for classroom discussions and activities and is also a tool for reflection after a discussion or other activity. Discussing ideas helps students recognize multiple perspectives, clarify their thinking, get answers to questions, and deepen their understanding. We provide several prompts that can be used to stimulate both journal writing and small-group or large-group discussions. These prompts do not have specific right or wrong answers; they are intended to help students think about complicated and important issues raised in the text—issues that have relevance in society today. Furthermore, while some prompts are focused on particular text or events in *Red Scarf Girl* and others are focused more on students' own ideas, experience, and prior knowledge, they are designed in combination to help students see connections between the text and their own lives. For specific ideas on different ways to structure classroom discussions or journal writing, refer to the Classroom Strategies link in the Educator Resources section of our website: *www.facinghistory.org*. (Note: in the ☑**TEACHING STRATEGIES** section, we have included comprehension questions for each chapter. These questions ask students to recall specific information from *Red Scarf Girl*, while the suggested journal and discussion questions are more interpretive.)

- **Using Documents:** In her memoir *Red Scarf Girl*, Ji-li Jiang provides a compelling account of her experience as a young adult growing up during the Cultural Revolution. While this memoir is informative, it presents only one perspective of this historical event. Facing History believes that for students to deeply understand the past, they need to investigate it from multiple perspectives. Therefore, to help students understand China and the Cultural Revolution, and to provide them with opportunities to develop the habit of analyzing events from different points of view, this study guide includes 19 documents. The documents include propaganda posters, photographs, poems, songs, excerpts from memoirs, government documents, and selections of quotations from people who lived during the Cultural Revolution. The Using Documents section explains the historical context of these documents and provides several ideas about how these resources might be used in the classroom.

- **Extensions:** This section provides a range of other activities to use to deepen students' understanding of the ideas and issues raised in *Red Scarf Girl*, as well as to enhance students' reading, writing, and critical-thinking skills. Because we know that students learn in different ways, our suggestions incorporate a wide range of activities, including drawing, speaking, movement, creative writing, and drama. We include several activities in each part, but you could certainly use these activities with a different section of the text.

At the end of each part, we have included **Documents** associated with that section of the guide. Although we have connected particular **Documents** to specific parts of the guide, we do not intend this structure to suggest that this is the only time when it would be appropriate to incorporate these **Documents**. The **Documents** could also be used before reading *Red Scarf Girl* as a way to introduce students to the history explored in the book, and many of the **Documents** could be paired with other chapters in *Red Scarf Girl*. For a complete list of **Documents**, see the main Table of Contents in the beginning of this guide.

At the back of this study guide, you will find a section called ☑ **TEACHING STRATEGIES**—auxiliary resources that can facilitate your teaching of *Red Scarf Girl*, such as comprehension questions for each chapter, a character chart, and an explanation of any of the teaching strategies we refer to in the study guide. For a complete list of teaching strategies, see the Table of Contents on page 113.

ASSESSMENT IDEAS

Here are several ways to evaluate students' comprehension and analysis of *Red Scarf Girl*, as well as to gauge their understanding of the Cultural Revolution and their ability to relate the ideas in this text to their own lives:

- Review students' responses to the journal prompts. Do they refer to specific evidence from the text? Do they offer several interpretations of what might be happening? Do they connect ideas from the text to their own lives? Do they raise questions?

- Listen to the questions and ideas students raise during class discussions. When they discuss the text, are they following the plot line? Can they refer to specific examples? Are they able to connect what is happening in the story to the larger historical context? Are students able to see connections between their own lives and issues in the text, while still appreciating how each historical moment is unique?

- Use essential questions as prompts for essay questions. For example, drawing from information about the Cultural Revolution (and text from *Red Scarf Girl*), other events in history, and their own experience, students could write an essay answering the question "What are the consequences for individuals and groups who are considered outside of society's universe of responsibility?" An extension of this essay might ask students to also reflect on who is included and excluded from their own universe of responsibility and to consider the implications of this choice. You could select several essential questions and allow students to respond to the one that most interests them.

- The activities suggested in the Using Documents section and the Extensions section lend themselves to assignments that could be evaluated for historical understanding, literary analysis, and students' ability to connect what they read to their own lives.

- Students could write a found poem about an important theme raised in *Red Scarf Girl*, such as conformity, universe of responsibility, or civic participation. To accompany their poem, students can write an "artist statement" in which they explain the message of their poem, why this message is meaningful to them, and how it relates to the Cultural Revolution. For more information about found poems, refer to page 121.

ADDITIONAL RESOURCES

Memoirs:

Many memoirs have been written about the Cultural Revolution. Some of these have not been translated and are not sold outside of China. Those most available to a Western audience have been written by Chinese, like Ji-li Jiang, who have immigrated to the United States or Britain. Some scholars have argued that because Western audiences typically only read accounts written by Chinese who have chosen to leave the country, Westerners have access to only unflattering accounts of the Cultural Revolution.[1]

For middle school readers, we suggest the following:

- *Revolution Is Not a Dinner Party*, by Ying Chang
- *China's Son*, by Da Chen
- *Snow Falling in Spring*, by Moying Li

For more advanced readers, we recommend:

- *Wild Swans*, by Jung Chang
- *Along the Roaring River*, by Hao Jiang Tian
- *Life and Death in Shanghai*, by Nien Cheng
- *Born Red*, by Gao Yuan

You could have students read another memoir and compare it to *Red Scarf Girl*. Or you could use these books to structure literature circles. For information about literature circles, see *http://www.facinghistory.org/resources/units/literature-circles-facing-history*.

Films:

- *China: A Century of Revolution* (especially part two), by filmmaker Sue Williams, *www.zeitgeistfilms.com*
- *Morning Sun*

Teachers in our network can borrow both of these films from the Facing History lending library.

Websites:

- "Ordinary Life in Extraordinary Times," *http://www.washington.edu/burkemuseum/ordinarylife/intro_new.html*
- "Morning Sun," *http://www.morningsun.org*
- "Discovering China," *http://library.thinkquest.org/26469/index2.html*
- "Chinese Posters," *http://chineseposters.net*

Academic Books:

- *The Chinese Cultural Revolution: A History*, by Paul Clark
- *Mao's Last Revolution*, by Roderick MacFarquhar and Michael Schoenhals
- *Modernization and Revolution in China: From the Opium Wars to the Olympics*, edited by Jay Cornin, June Grasso, and Michael Kort

---

[1] In the forward of Yarong Jiang and David Ashley's book *Mao's Children in the New China* (New York: Routledge, 2000), Stanley Rosen explains how the most widely read accounts of the Cultural Revolution portray this period as "oppressive" and "tragic." For positive accounts of the Cultural Revolution, see the following:

- Dongping Han, *The Unknown Cultural Revolution: Life and Change in a Chinese Village* (New York: Monthly Review Press, 2008).

- Mobo Gao, *The Battle for China's Past: Mao and the Cultural Revolution* (London: Pluto Press, 2008).

- Xueping Zhong, Wang Zheng, and Bai Di, eds., *Some of Us: Chinese Women Growing Up in the Mao Era* (New Brunswick, NJ: Rutgers University Press, 2001).

- Lincoln Cushing and Ann Tompkins, *Chinese Posters: Art from the Great Proletarian Cultural Revolution* (San Francisco, CA: Chronicle Books, 2007).

PRE-READING

Introducing *Red Scarf Girl* and the Cultural Revolution

OVERVIEW

Students develop a deeper understanding of history when they have the opportunity to connect themes from the past to events in the present and their own lives. Therefore, before beginning *Red Scarf Girl,* we recommend that students first explore and deepen their views about key themes that emerge in the text, such as conformity, obedience, revolution, responsibility, and equality. Introduction to these concepts now means that they will be familiar to students when encountered in *Red Scarf Girl.* For example, if students have already considered their own answer to the question "How do you create a fair society?" they are in a better position to recognize that one way in which many Chinese answered this question was through support of Chinese Communist Party ideals expressed through the Cultural Revolution.

In addition to familiarizing students with the broad themes addressed in *Red Scarf Girl,* preparing students to read the memoir also involves introducing its historical context. *Red Scarf Girl* begins in 1966 at the start of the Cultural Revolution in China. In order for students to understand Ji-li's experiences and to appreciate why so many Chinese youth were inspired to join the Cultural Revolution, it is critical that students have a basic grounding in the ideals expressed by Mao Zedong and the Chinese Communist Party (CCP). In this section, we have included documents aimed at helping students answer the questions "Why did the CCP appeal to millions of Chinese?" and "Why did they choose to follow Chairman Mao Zedong?" (For more information about the CCP, refer to the Using Documents section below.) A basic awareness of key terms that Jiang uses throughout her memoir, including Communist Party, class struggle, capitalists, reactionary, and bourgeois(ie), will also help students find the text more accessible. Fortunately, Jiang defines these terms, and others, in the glossary found at the back of the book. Students can use these definitions as a starting point as they construct their own understanding of the terms based on their experiences, beliefs, and prior knowledge. Also, on page xi, Jiang includes a "Note to the Reader" in which she explains the conventions relating to names in China. Of particular importance is the fact that in China, the last name typically precedes the first name. Thus, when Chinese refer to "Chairman Mao," they are not using his first name, as it might appear to students who are familiar with the name Mao Zedong.

Finally, before beginning to read *Red Scarf Girl,* we suggest that you discuss the strengths and weaknesses of the genre of memoir as a tool to learn about history. While memoirs provide a unique, personal window into the past, they represent only one experience. Encourage students to use the historical documents included with this study guide to broaden and deepen their understanding of the Cultural Revolution.

ESSENTIAL QUESTIONS

What is revolution? What is culture? What is a "cultural revolution"?

What are different reasons why people join revolutions and movements for social change?

How should resources be distributed in a society? How do societies achieve greater equality among their citizens? How do you create a fair society?

What is a memoir? How can memoirs help us understand the past?

SUGGESTED ACTIVITIES

DISCUSSIONS AND JOURNAL WRITING

Exploring culture and revolution

Based on your own experience and your knowledge of history, what are some examples of revolutions? Why have people joined revolutions, protests, and social movements? What are factors that might encourage you to participate in a revolution, protest, or social movement?

Mao Zedong, leader of the Communist revolution in China, wrote, "A revolution is not a dinner party, or writing an essay, or painting a picture, or doing embroidery; it cannot be so refined, so leisurely and gentle, so temperate, kind, and courteous, restrained and magnanimous. A revolution is an insurrection, an act of violence by which one class overthrows another." How is Chairman Mao defining revolution in this statement? Do you strongly agree, agree, disagree, or strongly disagree with Mao Zedong's ideas about revolution? Explain your answer. Then write your own definition of *revolution*.

Anthropologists are social scientists who study culture. What do you think they study? Some anthropologists define culture as the shared knowledge, beliefs, and behaviors of a group of people.[1] How would you describe the culture in which you live? What makes up or contributes to the culture of a society?

What does it mean for a culture to undergo a revolution? In a "cultural revolution," what do you think the revolutionaries might be trying to change? Identify a cultural revolution that impacted your community (local, national, or global). What changed as a result of this revolution?

Exploring equality, fairness, and society

In what ways is your society equal? In what ways do you think it is unequal? What could be done to increase equality in your community?

Many democratic nations, including the United States, define equality largely in terms of political rights. The Chinese Communist Party, led by Chairman Mao Zedong, defined equality largely in terms of economics—the kinds and quality of resources (e.g., land, money, property, education) citizens have access to. What kind of equality do you think is most important? Why? Is it possible for a society to achieve both economic and political equality? Explain your answer.

Are equality and fairness the same thing, or are they different? Identify an example of when achieving equality may be perceived as being unfair to some people. Identify an example of when achieving fairness may result in inequality. What should be done when values of fairness and equality are in conflict?

Exploring memoir

What is a memoir? Why do you think people write memoirs? If you were to write a memoir, what stories would you include? What stories would you leave out? Explain your decisions.

Is a memoir fiction or nonfiction? How do you know if what you are reading in a memoir is true? What is the difference between learning about a historical event through reading a memoir and learning about it through other sources, such as primary source documents or history books? What does a memoir provide that other sources do not? What might other sources provide that a memoir does not provide?

USING DOCUMENTS: THE CHINESE COMMUNIST PARTY (CCP)

The People's Republic of China was founded in 1949 based on a Communist vision of a classless society—a nation in which all individuals are equal in economic, social, and political power. Since 221 BCE, China had been ruled by a series of dynasties in which power passed down from one ruler to the next in the same family for generations. Throughout this period, a tiny and elite landlord class ruled over the masses of poor peasants. By 1900, Britain, Germany, Japan, and other countries exerted control over parts of China, and the imperial government continued the tradition of subjugating the peasant population. In 1912, China entered what historians refer to as the Modern Era, after a military uprising overthrew the Qing Dynasty that had been in power since 1644 and established the Republic of China. Although it seemed that power would finally rest with the people, in fact the country was politically unstable, and warlords fought to capture control of regions across China. The presence of international forces—especially the influence of Japan, which invaded China in the 1930s—served only to exacerbate the political instability of the Chinese republic.

Life for the peasants remained largely unchanged in the first decades of the twentieth century. However, it was also a period of intellectual freedom and debate that led to the emergence of various political movements, including the Chinese Communist Party (CCP). Founded in 1921, the Chinese Communist Party's idyllic vision of a classless and egalitarian society was particularly appealing to the vast majority of Chinese who had traditionally lacked any hope for social mobility. The CCP platform was fervently anti-Western, which appealed to Chinese who resented foreign influence over China. Still, the Communist Party struggled to gain power from local warlords. To unite China and defeat local warlords, in 1924, the Communists joined forces with the Nationalist Party, which was led by Sun Yat-sen and, later, Chiang Kai-shek. Chiang Kai-shek turned against the Communists and nearly wiped them out in a bloody purge in April 1927. Most of the surviving Communists retreated to safety in the countryside. In 1928, civil war ended as Chiang Kai-shek declared victory for the Nationalists. Chiang and the Nationalist Party took control of the government of the Republic of China and continued efforts to exterminate the Communist Party.

Mao Zedong emerged as one of the top leaders of the Chinese Communist Party when he led the CCP and its Red Army on what became known as the "Long March," a 6,000-mile retreat from the Nationalist Army to set up a strong base in the northwestern region of China. Thousands died along the way during this grueling trek, which started in 1934 and ended one year later. It was at this northwest base that Mao consolidated his power within the CCP and was elected chairman of the party.

Japan launched a full-scale invasion of China as part of military activity in the Asian arena shortly before World War II in 1937. The Japanese quickly took over the eastern part of the country, including major cities such as Beijing and Nanjing. To defeat the Japanese, the Nationalists and the Communists once again agreed to join forces. From their base in the northwest, the Communists gained popular support because of their strong resistance to the Japanese and their social and economic programs, including land reform. Shortly after Japan surrendered in 1945, civil war between the Communists and the Nationalists broke out. The Communists won an unexpectedly rapid and decisive victory, driving Chiang Kai-shek off the Chinese mainland to the island of Taiwan. On October 1, 1949, Chairman Mao Zedong proclaimed the founding of the People's Republic of China (PRC). Since then, the Chinese Communist Party has functioned as the only significant political party in the PRC and has controlled government policies, both foreign and domestic.

- **Document 1:** *Life in China Before the Communist Revolution (1949)*
- **Document 2:** *Rural Population in Xumwu County, Jiangxi Province, 1930*
- **Document 3:** *Policies Supported by the Chinese Communist Party*

These documents were selected in order to help students answer the following questions: What problems were the Chinese Communist Party (CCP), under the leadership of Chairman Mao, trying to solve? What ideas did they have about how to solve these problems? Why do you think many Chinese people supported the CCP? If students can answer these questions before they begin reading *Red Scarf Girl*, they will be in a better position to appreciate the choices made by Ji-li Jiang and the other characters in the book.

You could use the *jigsaw teaching strategy* to help structure this activity. Alternatively, you could distribute all three documents to students, individually or in groups, and ask them to use them to answer the question "Why do you think the Chinese people supported the CCP?"

EXTENSIONS

1. Previewing *Red Scarf Girl:* One way to introduce students to *Red Scarf Girl* is to give them 10 or 15 minutes to look over the book. Make sure students notice that the book includes a glossary, a pronunciation guide, and two images of the author. By looking at the cover, students might surmise that this story is about a young girl, and they might begin to guess her age. The preview activity might also ask students to locate China on a world map. Then students can also find Shanghai, where most of the story takes place. The *word wall teaching strategy* can help introduce students to new vocabulary they will encounter as they read *Red Scarf Girl*. Suggested words for your word wall include: *Communist Party, communism, People's Liberation Army, political background, class status, bourgeois(ie), capitalist/capitalism, revolutionary, counter-revolutionary, Chairman Mao Zedong, conservative, revolution, Cultural Revolution, proletarian, reactionary, revisionist, rightist, socialism*. Finally, in the ☑**TEACHING STRATEGIES** section, we have included a sample *anticipation guide*, designed to help students process their own opinions about conformity, obedience, loyalty, equality, and other important themes addressed in *Red Scarf Girl*.

2. **Using documentaries:** Showing a documentary about the history of modern China is an effective way to introduce students to the historical context of *Red Scarf Girl*. We recommend two documentaries. *China: A Century of Revolution* is a three-part series by filmmaker Sue Williams that explores the history of modern China. "The Mao Years," part two of this series, is especially relevant for readers of *Red Scarf Girl*. The first chapter of the film explains the founding of the People's Republic of China and highlights the extraordinary hope that millions of Chinese had in the Communist Party. Chapters 10–13 explore the Cultural Revolution in the years 1966–1968, the same years covered in *Red Scarf Girl*. We also recommend *Morning Sun*, an excellent film about the Cultural Revolution that includes footage of artistic productions, especially opera, and interviews with Chinese who came of age during the Cultural Revolution, much like Ji-li Jiang. Teachers in our network can borrow both of these films from the Facing History lending library.

3. **Timelines:** One way to help students understand the historical context for *Red Scarf Girl* is through a **human timeline activity**. You can use the timelines we have included in this study guide, or you could have students create their own timelines. They can gather historical information for their timelines by:

- Watching a documentary about China; see the "Using Documentaries" section above for suggested films.

- Researching on the Internet; the following websites provide useful background information about modern Chinese history and the Cultural Revolution:

  - "Ordinary Life in Extraordinary Times" (*www.washington.edu/burkemuseum/ordinarylife/intro_new.html*) is an online exhibit developed by the Burke Museum of Natural History and Culture at University of Washington. This well-organized exhibit includes detailed historical information about the Cultural Revolution and images of artifacts from the period.

  - The Morning Sun website (*www.morningsun.org*) draws from a wide array of resources, from music to images to primary source documents, in order to represent the complex history of the Cultural Revolution.

- The Discovering China website (*library.thinkquest.org/26469*), designed by students, provides information about China's history before the Cultural Revolution and has more detailed background about the Cultural Revolution. This site also includes interactive features such as online quizzes and polls.

- Taking notes during a lecture; the historical overview written by Professor William A. Joseph, as well as the timelines on pages 140–143, can provide the basic structure for a lecture.

---

[1] For definitions of *culture*, see "What is Culture?" Center for Advanced Research on Language Acquisition website, *http://www.carla.umn.edu/culture/definitions.html* (accessed June 4, 2009).

DOCUMENT 1

Life in China Before the Communist Revolution (1949)

Quotation #1: A conversation with a poor peasant (1921)

When I asked him how things were with him, he just shook his head. "In a very bad way. Even my sixth [child] can do a little work, but still we haven't enough to eat . . . and then there is no security . . . all sorts of people want money, there is no fixed rule . . . and the harvests are bad. You grow things, and when you take them to sell you always have to pay several taxes and lose money, while if you don't try to sell, the things might go bad . . ."[1]

Quotation #2: Description of life in a section of Shanghai where wealthy Chinese landowners, officials, and business owners lived (1920)

Both sides of the road are filled with handsome cars, quietly waiting for their masters' bidding after playing tennis or when leaving supper clubs. . . . The electric lights come on. . . . Evening meals begin. In the kitchens, the sounds of basins, pots, bowls, bells, dining rooms with the sound of music, wine glasses being clinked.[2]

Quotation #3: An excerpt from the memoir of the son of a wealthy government official

I was born in 1940. Until I was five, I lived in Father's giant mansion in Nanjing. . . . Behind the mansion were two separate buildings that housed an enormous kitchen and the living quarters for more than a dozen servants. . . . It was customary in those days for wealthy Chinese children to be given to the care of wet nurses. . . . The living quarters I shared with my nanny were located in one wing of the mansion. We had two rooms with our own bedroom, plus the balcony where I spent so much time. "Nai-ma" [milk mother] was not my nanny's actual name—it was a literal title for what she did. I never knew her real name. . . . Many years later, I learned that when she took on the job of being my milk mother a month after my birth, she had just given birth to her own child. In order to take the job to earn an income for her family, she left the baby behind in the village. It had to be heart wrenching for her.[3]

Quotation #4: Description of peasant life in China (1922)

*The inside of all thatched-roof farm homes were the same: black rafters, gray walls, a dirt floor, a kitchen table, a bench, farm **implements**, and **amulets** from the local temple. There was generally nothing on the walls, rather more well-off families might have several advertisements . . . stuck on the wall. The floors were covered with chicken [feces], and people walked through it with their bare feet. Amid such conditions, the popular saying in the area: "Nothing to eat, nothing to wear—those things still go to the little king [the name farmers in the area gave to landlords]."[4]*

Quotation #5: Description of an attempt to form peasant unions (1921–1923)

I found myself back at the village where I had visited the day before. This time, I encountered a peasant of forty, who asked me, "Sir, are you here to collect land rent?"

"No, no, I am here to help you collect your due. Someone owes you money, and you've forgotten it. I'm here to remind you."

"What!" the man exclaimed. "I'll be lucky not to owe others money. Who'd owe anything to me?"

"Don't you know?" I told him. "The landlords owe you a lot. Year in and year out, they sit at home and do nothing, and you work in the fields until you drop dead. In the end they are the ones who get the yields as rent. The piece of land worth at most one hundred dollars has been tilled by you for a hundred, a thousand years—and how much grain have you submitted to the landlords? We think it's really unfair. That's why I'm here to talk with you, to find out a way to get even with the landlords."

The man smiled and said, "That'll be great indeed! But we will be locked up and beaten up if we only owe them a pint or a tenth of a pint. Such is fate—those who collect rent always collect rent, and those who till the fields always till the fields. Good day, sir. I've got to go to town."[5]

Quotation #6: Description of the typical diet of a peasant, taken from a study of a Chinese village published in 1945

*Among the poor, sweet potatoes are eaten at every meal every day throughout the year. From harvest time until the spring of the following year, they eat fresh sweet potatoes; when these are gone, they eat the stored dry slices. . . . **Supplementing** the potatoes are, first, a kind of gruel made of barley flour and peanut powder; second, a kind of hash made of chopped turnips and soybean juice; and third, one or two kinds of pickles. Occasionally, some kind of bread is served.[6]*

Quotation #7: The daughter of a wealthy businessman describes her home in Shanghai

Father's Shanghai house was on Avenue Joffre . . . Father led us into a charming garden, with a small lane lined by cropped camellia bushes, a magnolia tree, wonderfully fragrant blooms, and a wishing well. . . . "Here we are!" Father said, looking around proudly as we gawked in open-mouthed wonder at the burgundy velvet couches, matching velvet curtains, and thin woolen carpet partially covering a *teak parquet floor. The wallpaper had strips of raised velvet **napping** that matched the curtains. . .*

Niang entered, holding Fourth Brother's hand. . . . Like the room, our stepmother was also stylish and flawless, with large, piercing eyes, long shapely nails painted bright red, and enormous flashing diamonds at her throat, wrist, and ears. . . . "We have enrolled you at very expensive private missionary schools. School starts next Monday. Now go with the maids to your rooms and wash yourselves. In half an hour, Cook will ring the dinner bell."[7]

GLOSSARY

amulets: objects or charms believed to have magical powers to protect the person who wears them

implements: tools

napping: decoration created by a raised surface of yarn or fabric

supplementing: in addition to

teak parquet: a floor made from teak wood, considered very elegant and expensive

[1] Patricia Buckley Ebrey, *Chinese Civilization: A Sourcebook*. ed. P.B. Ebrey, 2nd ed. (The Free Press, 1993), 358.

[2] R. Keith Schoppa, *Twentieth Century China: A History in Documents* (Oxford University Press, 2004), 67.

[3] Charles N. Li, *The Bitter Sea: Coming of Age in a China Before Mao* (Harper Collins, 2009), 18–27.

[4] Ibid., 67.

[5] Ebrey, Op. cit., 366.

[6] Martin C. Yang, *A Chinese Village: Taitou, Shantung Province* (Columbia University Press, 1945), 32.

[7] Adeline Yen Mah, *Chinese Cinderella: The True Story of an Unwanted Daughter* (Delacorte Press, 1999), 23–25.

DOCUMENT 2

Rural Population in Xumwu County, Jiangxi Province, 1930[1]

The Chinese Communist Party wanted to know more about how **rural** society was structured, so that it could plan its land reform policy. This chart represents the results of a survey conducted between 1920 and 1930.

Note: landlords are defined as those who own land that is farmed by peasants. Typically, landlords collected food as payment for the use of this land. Wealthy landlords might have collected more than 30 tons of rice per year, while minor landlords might have collected less than 10 tons of rice per year.

GROUP	PERCENT OF COUNTY POPULATION
Wealthy landlords	0.045%
Middle-class landlords	0.4%
Minor landlords	3%
Rich peasants (defined as those who have some **surplus** food)	4%
Middle peasants (defined as those who have just enough food for their families)	18%
Poor peasants (defined as those who do not have **sufficient** food to feed their families and typically have taken out loans)	70%
Manual workers and craftsman (i.e., tailors, porters)	3%
Loafers (defined as those who have no land and no work)	1%

GLOSSARY

rural: the country; not the people or cultures near a city

sufficient: an amount that is just enough for survival; not too much or too little

surplus: an amount that is more than needed for survival

---

[1] Schoppa, *Twentieth Century China: A History in Documents* (Routledge, 2002), 95.

DOCUMENT 3

Policies Supported by the Chinese Communist Party

The Chinese Communist Party (CCP) was founded in 1921. One of the CCP's guiding principles was that the peasants and working class, who made up the vast majority of the Chinese population, were being **exploited** by landowners, government officials, military officers, and other members of the "upper class." The CCP believed that if resources were more equally distributed, China would be more prosperous. Two important policies the party introduced concerned land reform and marriage. Both of these policies fundamentally changed Chinese society by giving more power to traditionally powerless groups: women, peasants, and the working class.

Excerpt of Land Reform Law Proposed by the Communist Party (1932)[1]

Laws that pertain to what land should be confiscated:

1. Land (including land rented to tenants), houses, and all other forms of property, including household items, that belong to members of the **gentry** and landlords are to be confiscated.

2. Land, houses, and all other forms of property, including household items that belong to the family **shrines**, Buddhist or Daoist temples, [or] clan or social organizations are to be confiscated.

3. Land owned by rich peasants should be confiscated.

Laws that pertain to who should receive land:

1. The amount of land to be distributed is the same for all **tenant farmers** and poor peasants. . . .

2. The relatives of a farm laborer shall receive land. . . .

3. Independent **artisans**, . . . physicians, and teachers are to receive land if they have been unemployed for six months or longer.

4. Shop owners and their relatives shall not receive any land.

5. Rich peasants will receive poor land. . . .

6. . . . Members of the gentry, landlords, and members of counter-revolutionary organizations will not be entitled to land distribution. . . .

14. A woman can **dispose** of her land the way she wishes when she is married.

The Marriage Law of 1950[2]

Article I: The **feudal** marriage system, which is based on **arbitrary** and **compulsory** arrangement, and the superiority of man over woman, and ignores the children's interests, shall be abolished.

The New Democratic marriage system, which is based on the free choice of partners, on **monogamy**, on equal rights for both sexes, and on the protection of the lawful interests of women and children, shall be put into effect.

GLOSSARY

arbitrary: random or illogical

artisans: craftsman, such as tailors or shoe makers

compulsory: required, often by law

dispose: to get rid of

exploited: to have been used or treated unfairly for the benefit of another person

feudal: a system where power and wealth are controlled by a few "elite" people, who then have control of the lives of the poor majority

gentry: the elite or upper class

monogamy: the practice of marrying only one person

shrines: sacred places for the worship of a god or an ancestor

tenant farmers: farmers who rent land and pay the landowner with a portion of their crops

---

[1] Schoppa, *Twentieth Century China: A History in Documents* (Routledge, 2002), 95.

[2] Ibid., 96–98.

PART 1: CHANGING CULTURE, SHIFTING IDENTITIES

Includes the Prologue through chapter "Writing *Da–zi–bao*"
(pp. 1–51)

OVERVIEW

While the historical context of China between 1964 and 1975 is certainly unique, the themes that emerge in the first several chapters of *Red Scarf Girl* are universal and can provide a point of resonance for many students as they navigate their own moral universe. Identity is one significant theme introduced in these first chapters. When we first meet the memoir's narrator, Ji-li, she is "the luckiest girl in the world." There is a "sweet breeze" in the air as Ji-li describes her happy life, including her powerful loyalty to Chairman Mao. By the end of the third chapter, "ghostly shadows" fill the "darkness," symbolizing that Ji-li's luck, and identity, are changing.

Like Ji-li, many teenagers are concerned with questions of identity and belonging. The issues raised in *Red Scarf Girl* can help students consider questions they confront in their own lives: Who am I? How do I define myself? How am I defined by others? To which groups do I belong? From which groups am I excluded? Our answers to these questions shape the decisions we make as individuals in society. For example, in these first chapters of *Red Scarf Girl*, we read about several moments when Ji-li conforms, sometimes willingly and sometimes reluctantly, to group behavior. Analyzing these situations can provoke important discussions about peer pressure, the power of groupthink, and the risks associated with dissent.

The first sign that Ji-li's life is about to change is when her father says she cannot audition for a place in the Central Liberation Army Arts Academy. She does not fully understand the problems with her political background that keep her from pursuing this opportunity. Indeed, her father asserts, "It's very complicated, and you wouldn't understand it now even if I told you." Still, despite her lack of understanding, she reluctantly follows her father's wishes. Holding back her tears, Ji-li hands her principal a note from her father explaining that she cannot participate in the auditions. The moment when Ji-li hands the principal the note from her father foreshadows Ji-li's shifting identity—from that of the "Outstanding Student" and "*da-dui-zhang*, the student chairman of the whole school," to that of the "black whelp" and "capitalist roader" that she is labeled later in the story.*

This moment marks the first of many choices Ji-li is forced to make as a teenager growing up during the Cultural Revolution. In Chapter 2, Ji-li begins to decide how she wants to participate in revolutionary actions designed to rid China of the Four Olds. Demolishing store signs may be exciting, but she bends down and pretends to tie her shoelaces when her aunt is publicly humiliated. In Chapter 3, Ji-li faces a dilemma when she is supposed to write a *da-zi-bao* (big character poster) denigrating her teachers. As the memoir progresses, the consequences of Ji-li's decision become more significant for

---

* In *Red Scarf Girl*, Ji-li Jiang recounts how she was called a "black whelp" and how she fears being labeled one of the "five black categories." This reflects common language used during the Cultural Revolution, where "black" denoted a negative political label, not a racial term. In other words, labeling someone as "black" was an accusation of anti-party sentiment and counterrevolutionary behavior. It was not representative of a racist attitude based on skin color or ethnicity. You may want to clarify this point for students who are likely unfamiliar with this usage of the word "black."

her safety and the safety of her family. Her situation was not exceptional. The Cultural Revolution created conditions where many Chinese were forced to decide among loyalties to state, family, friends, and self. Through its analysis of how Ji-li's loyalties shift over time, *Red Scarf Girl* provides the opportunity for students to reflect on their own "universe of responsibility"—the people and groups whom they feel an obligation to care for and protect.

ESSENTIAL QUESTIONS

What is identity? To what extent do we define ourselves? To what extent are we defined by others?

How do individuals, groups, and nations decide who to include in their "universe of responsibility"—the people whom they feel an obligation to care for and protect? What are the consequences for individuals and groups who are considered outside of a community's universe of responsibility?

What is a cultural revolution? What strategies can be used to change a community's culture?

SUGGESTED ACTIVITIES

DISCUSSIONS AND JOURNAL WRITING

For Chapter 1:

On page 1, Ji-li recites this Chinese saying popular in the 1960s: "Heaven and Earth are great, but greater still is the kindness of the Communist Party; father and mother are dear, but dearer still is Chairman Mao."

What do you think the above quotation means? What does it tell you about the relationship between the Chinese and their political leaders at the time? How does this compare to your own relationship to government leaders?

Individuals, groups, and nations have a group of people to whom they feel a sense of loyalty, or whom they feel a sense of responsibility to care for and protect. Facing History refers to this concept as one's "universe of responsibility." At this point in the memoir, who do you think Ji-li includes in her universe of responsibility? To whom does she feel the greatest sense of responsibility or loyalty? Who do you include in your universe of responsibility?

How would you describe the sense of loyalty and responsibility you feel toward government leaders (e.g., very strong, strong, weak . . .)? Toward your country? What do you think instills a sense of patriotism in young people?

For Chapter 2:

On page 25, Ji-li says, "But Grandma, we have to get rid of those old ideas, old culture, old customs, and old habits. Chairman Mao said they're holding us back." What are some examples of Four Olds provided in this chapter? Do you think old ideas, culture, customs, or habits have the power to hold people back? Why or why not?

Identify an example from history or from your own experience of an old idea or custom that has held people back. Then identify an example of a tradition or habit that has benefited society. How do we know when a tradition or "old idea" should be discarded and when the tradition or idea should be preserved?

Reflecting on the importance of ridding China of the Four Olds, Ji-li asserts, "Though we were not facing real guns or real tanks, this battle would be even harder, because our enemies, the rotten ideas and customs we were so used to, were inside ourselves" (pp. 28–29). Do you strongly agree, agree, disagree, or strongly disagree with Ji-li's statement? How do we combat an enemy that is "inside ourselves"? Have you ever successfully stopped a way of thinking or a habit? If so, what did you need to do to make this change possible?

For Chapter 3:

In the chapter "Writing *Da-zi-bao*," students complain about the lack of fairness in the education system. What are some of their arguments? Do you agree or disagree with these ideas? If you were to design a school that is fair to all students, what would it be like?

When Ji-li is placed in a group of students who are given the task of humiliating her aunt, Ji-li says, "I had no choice but to go" (p. 45). Do you agree with her assessment of the situation? What range of options, if any, was available to her? What might have been the consequences of making a different choice? Identify a time when you felt like you had "no choice." Looking back at this situation, do you still feel as if you had "no choice"? Why or why not?

After Ji-li reads the *da-zi-bao* written about her, she cries, "It's all lies" (p. 51). How would someone know if the information on a *da-zi-bao* is true or false? How do you know if what you read is true or false?

Compare Ji-li's reaction during three "revolutionary" moments in this section: 1) observing the crowd tear down signs that represented the Four Olds (pp. 21–25); 2) watching the crowd tear a man's pants and destroy his shoes (pp. 30–33); and 3) joining with her peers in the humiliation of Aunt Xi-wen (pp. 44–48). How does she feel during each of these moments? If all of these examples represent ways to support Mao and the revolution, how might you explain Ji-li's different emotional reactions to these events?

USING DOCUMENTS: DESTROY THE OLD AND ESTABLISH THE NEW

Background[1]

The Cultural Revolution in China began with an aggressive campaign to "Destroy the Old and Establish the New." In August 1966, Chairman Mao authorized the Red Guards and all those loyal to the Communist Party to seek out and destroy the Four Olds—old ideas, old culture, old customs, and old habits. The campaign was another phase in the ongoing Cultural Revolution in China. Keeping the revolutionary spirit alive meant remaining vigilant for any sign of Western influence, religious worship, or evidence of wealth. Big character posters (*da-zi-bao*)* were plastered over city walls and buildings, repeating slogans from Chairman Mao or denouncing certain members of society as "capitalist roaders" unfaithful to the Communist Party and the People's Republic. Buildings were torn down or renamed, religious icons and books were burned, and homes were ransacked in an effort to purge society of counterrevolutionary thoughts and actions. Chairman Mao's words were used to legitimize these violent acts. This often-quoted Mao statement exemplifies how violence was associated in a positive way with being revolutionary:

> *A revolution is not a dinner party, or writing an essay, or painting a picture, or doing embroidery; it cannot be so refined, so leisurely and gentle, so temperate, kind, courteous, restrained and magnanimous. A revolution is an insurrection, an act of violence by which one class overthrows another.*"[2]

- **Document 4:** *Propaganda poster: "Bombard the Capitalist Headquarters"*

- **Document 5:** *"Smash the Four Olds," photographs*

- **Document 6:** *"Red Guards Destroy the Old and Establish the New," excerpt of a newspaper article published in the Peking Review, No. 36, September 2, 1966*

In the first chapters of *Red Scarf Girl*, Ji-li describes her involvement in the "Destroy the Old and Establish the New" campaign. The documents listed above provide specific details about this campaign. Students can use a graphic organizer, like the Document Analysis Form included in the ☑**TEACHING STRATEGIES** section of this guide, to record information from each of these sources. Before reviewing these documents, students can search through the first three chapters of *Red Scarf Girl*, identifying information about the Four Olds campaign. Then they can interpret the three Four Olds documents. How do these documents support Ji-li's description of what was happening in her neighborhood? What new information do they provide? These are questions students can answer in small groups. This exercise also provides an opportunity for students to discuss the validity of sources. Questions you can use to guide a discussion include: Which document—the poster, photography, newspaper article, or *Red Scarf Girl*—do you think provides the most truthful account of the Four Olds campaign? Why might

---

* *Da-zi-bao* are large handwritten posters typically mounted on walls and in other public spaces. They have been used in China as a tool for communication, protest, and propaganda for centuries. With rising literacy rates in the twentieth century, their use increased; it peaked during the Cultural Revolution, when they were often used to humiliate and denounce those suspected of being counterrevolutionary.

some types of sources appear more valid than others? Historians often rely on multiple types of sources, including photographs, newspaper articles, diary entries, government documents, and art, when trying to understand what happened in the past. Why might historians think it is important to gather information from different kinds of sources? What do you think? How has reviewing four different sources affected your understanding of the "Destroy the Old and Establish the New" campaign?

EXTENSIONS

1. **Identity charts:** Have students create an identity chart for Ji-li. Encourage students to include quotations from the text on their identity charts. (For more information about identity charts, refer to page 128.) Students can also contribute ideas to a class version of an identity chart that you can keep on the classroom wall. Reviewing this identity chart after each reading assignment is one way to help students keep track of how Ji-li changes throughout the novel. It also can provide an opportunity to discuss characterization with students. You might ask students to list the different ways that they learn about the main character, such as through physical description, actions, what she says, how she feels, and how other characters respond to her. To emphasize the point that identity is shaped by internal and external forces, you might have students construct a three-dimensional identity box rather than a two-dimensional chart. Inside the box, students can record ideas and quotations that describe how Ji-li defines her own identity. On the outside of the box, students can record ideas and quotations that describe how others are defining Ji-li. Students can add to their identity boxes for Ji-li as they read her memoir.

2. **Reader's theater:** Reader's theater is an activity designed to help students interpret text beyond the literal level. In this activity, groups of students are assigned a small portion of the text to present to their peers. Unlike the performance of skits to recap events in a story, reader's theater asks students to plan a performance that reveals the message, conflict, or theme that the author is trying to convey. Reader's theater is an effective way to help students process dilemmas that characters, especially Ji-li, experience throughout this memoir. The chapter "Writing *Da-zi-bao*" provides several moments that are appropriate for reader's theater. For example, groups could be assigned the following moments to present: 1) when Ji-li can't decide what to write on her *da-zi-bao* (pp. 38–39); 2) when Ji-li reads Yin Lan-lan's *da-zi-bao* (p. 40–middle of p. 42); 3) when Ji-li decides to write her *da-zi-bao* (pp. 42–43); 4) when Ji-li joins the group to denounce her aunt (pp. 44–45); 5) when Du-Hai denounces Aunt Xi-wen (pp. 46–47); and 6) when a *da-zi-bao* is written about Ji-li (pp. 48–51). For a detailed description of reader's theater, refer to page 130.

3. **Relationship webs:** Because many students are not familiar with the Chinese names in this book, keeping track of characters can prove challenging. A relationship web is a tool that can help students chart the connections among the characters in a book. As the main character, Ji-li should be placed in the center of the web. Students add additional characters to their web by drawing lines between the character's name and another character's name. On the connecting line, students should describe the relationship

between those two characters (e.g., friend, brother, teacher, adversary, political leader, etc.). Another way to help students keep track of the many characters in *Red Scarf Girl* is by completing a character chart—a graphic organizer in which students record information about characters in a novel. The ☑**TEACHING STRATEGIES** section includes a sample character chart for use with this memoir.

4. Story timeline: Creating a story timeline can help students keep track of the plot and align what is happening in *Red Scarf Girl* to events from modern Chinese history. If you have already constructed a timeline of modern Chinese history and/or the Cultural Revolution, you can record key moments from *Red Scarf Girl* directly on this timeline.

---

[1] "Destroy the Four Olds," The Association for Asian Studies website,
http://www. aasianst.org/EAA/10-3%20Supplemental/Handout-3.pdf (accessed June 4, 2009).
"Smash the Old World!" Morning Sun website, *http://www.morningsun.org/smash/pr9_1966.html* (accessed June 4, 2009).

[2] "Report On an Investigation of the Peasant Movement in Hunan" (March 1927), Selected Works, Vol. I, p. 28.

Propaganda poster: "Bombard the Capitalist Headquarters"

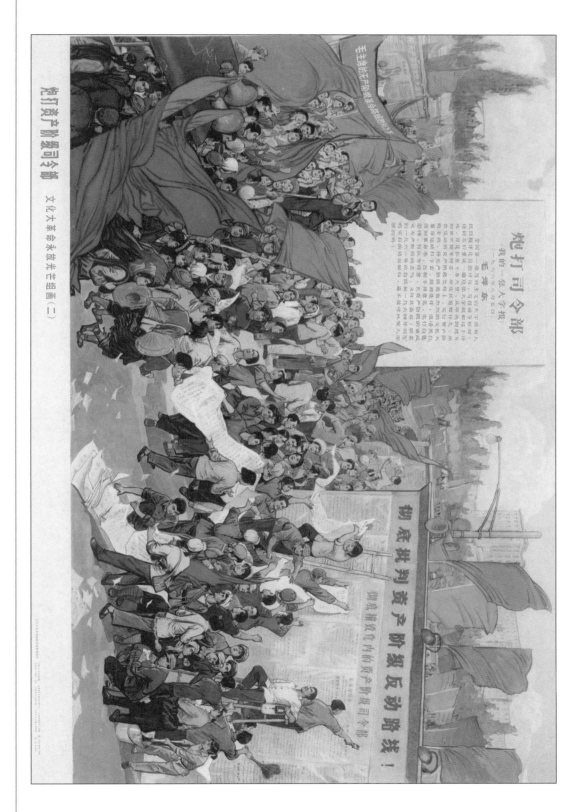

DOCUMENT 5

"Smash the Four Olds," photographs

DOCUMENT 6

"Red Guards Destroy the Old and Establish the New," excerpt from a newspaper article published in the *Peking Review*, 1966

*Since August 20, the young Red Guards of Peking [Beijing] . . . have taken to the streets. With the revolutionary rebel spirit of the **proletariat**, they have launched a furious offensive to sweep away **reactionary**, **decadent**, **bourgeois**, and **feudal** influences, and all old ideas, culture, customs, and habits. This mounting revolutionary storm is sweeping the cities of the entire nation. "Let Mao Tse-tung's thought occupy all positions; use it to transform the mental outlook of the whole of society; sweep away all ghosts and monsters; brush aside all stumbling-blocks and **resolutely** carry the great proletarian cultural revolution through to the end!" This is the militant aim of the young revolutionary fighters. Their revolutionary actions have everywhere received the enthusiastic support of the revolutionary masses.*

In Peking

*During the past week, more Red Guards have scored victory after victory as they pressed home their attack against the decadent customs and habits of the exploiting classes. Beating drums and singing revolutionary songs, detachments of Red Guards are out in the streets doing propaganda work, holding aloft big portraits of Chairman Mao, extracts from Chairman Mao's works, and great banners with the words: We are the critics of the old world; we are the builders of the new world. They have held street meetings, put up big-character posters, and distributed leaflets in their attack against all the old ideas and habits of the exploiting classes. As a result of the proposals of the Red Guards, and with the support of the revolutionary masses, shop signs which spread **odious** feudal and bourgeois ideas have been removed, and the names of many streets, lanes, parks, buildings, and schools **tainted** with **feudalism**, **capitalism**, or **revisionism**, or which had no revolutionary significance, have been replaced by revolutionary names.*

*The service trades have thrown out **obsolete** rules and regulations. Support for the revolutionary actions of the Red Guards has been expressed in countless big-character posters, which the masses of revolutionary workers and staff have put up in the newly renamed major **thoroughfares** of the capital. They have also expressed their support with street demonstrations. . . .*

In Shanghai

*In this huge city, which has the largest concentration of **capitalists** in the country and which, until the **liberation**, had long been under the rule of the **imperialists** and domestic **reactionaries**, the revolutionary students and the broad masses of workers and staff have taken up their iron brooms to sweep away all old habits and customs.*

*The show windows of the Wing On Co., one of the biggest department stores in the city, are plastered with big–character posters put up by the Red Guards and workers and staff of the store, proposing that "Wing On" ("Eternal Peace") should be changed into "Yong Hong" ("Red For Ever") or "Yong Dou" ("Struggle For Ever"). The posters point out that in the old society, the boss of the store chose the name "Wing On" because he wanted to be left in peace forever to exploit the working people. "For a long time now, the store has been in the hands of the people and we are certainly not going to tolerate this **odious** name a day longer," say the posters.*

In "The Great World," the biggest amusement centre of Shanghai, workers and staff together with the Red Guards took down the old name sign which was several meters long. When the last character of the sign was brought down, thousands of revolutionary people in the streets and in the windows of neighboring buildings applauded and cheered: "Long live Chairman Mao!" and "Long live the great proletarian cultural revolution!" . . .

*The revolutionary workers and staff of Shanghai barbershops have adopted revolutionary measures in response to the proposals of the Red Guards: they no longer cut and set hair in the grotesque fashions indulged in by a small minority of people; they cut out those services specially worked out for the **bourgeoisie**, such as manicuring, beauty treatments and so on. In those shops which sold only goods catering to the needs of a small minority of people, workers and staff have taken the revolutionary decision to start supplying the people at large with good popular **commodities** at low prices. . . .*

GLOSSARY

bourgeois(ie): middle-class people, often shopkeepers and landlords

capitalists: those who believe that people should be left to control the economy, even if it results in inequality between the rich and the poor

commodities: goods that people need on a day-to-day basis, such as food and clothing

decadent: having many unnecessary luxuries

feudal: a system where power and wealth are in the hands of a few elite people, who then have control of the lives of the poor majority

feudalism, capitalism, and revisionism: these movements were seen as enemies of the Chinese Communist Party because they do not support the main principle of communism: that wealth should be distributed evenly throughout the population

imperialists: those who believe that foreign countries should have power over China

liberation: this refers to the founding of the People's Republic of China by the Communist Party in 1949

obsolete: outdated

odious: disgusting and offensive

proletariat: working-class people, often farmers or factory workers

reactionaries: people opposed to change or revolution

reactionary: anything that is opposed to change or the revolution

resolutely: with certainty and a sense of purpose

tainted: influenced

thoroughfares: streets

PART 2: INCLUSION AND EXCLUSION

Includes "The Red Successors" (pp. 52–71), "Graduation"
(pp. 72–79), and "The Sound and Drums of Gongs" (pp. 80–99)

OVERVIEW

Look at any society or community, past or present, and you can observe how people are organized into smaller groups. Often, group membership is determined voluntarily as individuals seek relationships with people who share their interests, beliefs, goals, or backgrounds. Sometimes, membership in groups is not left to individual choice. People can be born into groups, such as a racial or gender group or a family. During the Cultural Revolution in China, family background or class status determined the groups to which an individual belonged. In Chapter 4 of *Red Scarf Girl*, we learn how Ji-li Jiang is excluded from membership in the Red Successors because of her family background. Most adolescents have experiences being included and excluded from groups—experiences that they can use to help them make sense of what is happening in the life of Ji-li Jiang during the Cultural Revolution.

As we read in *Red Scarf Girl*, during the Cultural Revolution, the Red Guards emerged as an important social group for young people. In late spring of 1966, Red Guard groups started to form across China's university and middle school campuses as a reaction to an article exposing bourgeois tendencies in the Communist Party.* Chairman Mao immediately expressed his support for the Red Guards, resulting in the growth of Red Guard groups throughout China. Former Red Guards offer different reasons for becoming Red Guards. For some, like Lu Xin, their motivation was ideologically driven. "When the Cultural Revolution began, I immediately became a Red Guard. . . . We saw the Cultural Revolution as an ideological struggle between right and wrong," she stated.[1] Another former Red Guard recalls how he joined "out of self-interest." "I wanted to belong, and I was personally ambitious," he said.[2] Wu Shanren, a former Red Guard, recalls that the Cultural Revolution "was the happiest period of my life."[3] He explains, "The Cultural Revolution opened another world for me. My painting and calligraphy skills were immediately put to good use."[4] Many Chinese youth were also excited to become Red Guards because their ideas, skills, and energy could be "put to good use."[5]

For Chinese youth, membership in the Red Guards represented belonging to the revolution and being accepted by Chinese society. In Chapter 4, we read about Ji-li's excitement to become one of the Red Successors, the version of Red Guards for younger students. After being nominated for this position, a position she wanted more than anything else, she shares how she was then denied entry because her grandfather was a landlord. "Those who don't have good class backgrounds shouldn't be elected," declares one student (p. 57). Indeed, inclusion in Chinese society during the Cultural Revolution was largely determined by class status. The revolutionary leaders classified people according to the Five Red or the Five Black categories based on their family background and ideological behavior. Landlords, rich farmers, anti-revolutionaries,

---

* In China, "middle school" is the level of education between elementary school and university. In many other countries, including the
  United States, this level of schooling is referred to as secondary school or high school.

criminals, and rightists made up the Five Blacks, while the Five Red categories consisted of revolutionary cadres, revolutionary martyrs, revolutionary soldiers, workers, and peasants. According to Professor Xing Lu, "During the Cultural Revolution, one's class status became the criterion for drawing lines between enemies and friends, and indeed, between good and evil."[6] Hao Jiang Tian grew up in China during the Cultural Revolution and admits that at that time, "No one wanted to have a so-called counterrevolutionary in their midst."[7]

Many individuals received "black" labels, including Ji-li's family, despite their loyalty to Chairman Mao and the People's Republic of China. In China, not only was the practice of labeling people as "red" or "black" misleading, but it also resulted in serious consequences for those who were deemed as less worthy because of their family background. The house searches described in Chapter 6 foreshadow more serious consequences that appear later in the story. As students will learn, belonging to the wrong social class not only invited house searches but also brought about ostracism, loss of jobs, humiliation, and even torture or death. Recognizing the significance of belonging to the wrong class, the Jiang family takes efforts to hide its family background, painting over antique trunks and turning silk dresses into mops.

At this point in the story, interpreting the actions of Ji-li and her family reveals the lengths that people are willing to go to in order to fit in to mainstream society. Reading about Ji-li's struggle to be included despite her family background provides an opportunity for students to reflect on their own experiences with membership, belonging, conformity, and ostracism. Studying the Cultural Revolution also helps students understand a recurring phenomenon throughout history: how the categorization of people into distinct and fixed groups often leads to prejudice and discrimination. While class status was used during the Cultural Revolution to create distinctions between "us" and "them," other societies have used class status, as well as race, religion, gender, and nationality, to establish membership in civic or social groups.

ESSENTIAL QUESTIONS

To what extent do we define ourselves? To what extent are we defined by others? How is identity shaped by the culture in which we live?

How do groups determine who belongs and who does not belong? What is the most appropriate and fair way to determine membership in a particular group? Under what conditions, if any, is it appropriate to exclude someone from membership in a group?

What are the consequences for individuals and groups who are considered outside of society's universe of responsibility?

What is a stereotype? What encourages stereotypes? What prevents or breaks down stereotypes? How does stereotyping individuals lead to prejudice and discrimination?

SUGGESTED ACTIVITIES

DISCUSSIONS AND JOURNAL WRITING

For chapter 4, "The Red Successors," pp. 52–71

When Ji-li's father talks to her about their family background, he says, "What I want you to know is, whether or not your Grandpa was a landlord or an exploiter, it isn't your responsibility. . . . [I]t isn't your fault. You didn't do anything wrong" (p. 63). Do you agree or disagree with his comments? Why do you think students are blaming Ji-li for her family background?

Some students, like Yu Jian, are judged positively because of their family backgrounds. The following saying was popular during the Cultural Revolution: "The son is a hero if the father is a revolutionary. The son is a rotten egg if the father is a counterrevolutionary."[7] Do you agree or disagree with this statement? Do you think it is fair or appropriate to use family background to judge someone in a positive or negative way? Explain your answers.

"It was so unfair. I was being punished for something I had not done," declares Ji-li (p. 70). Have you ever been punished or held responsible for something you did not do? How did it feel? How do you think Ji-li might be feeling at this moment?

On page 67, Ji-li says, "I had always been a school leader, a role model. How could I have suddenly become so bad that I needed to be remolded thoroughly?" How do you think Ji-li has changed since the beginning of this memoir (and the beginning of the Cultural Revolution)? Do you agree with Ji-li's opinion that she had "become bad"? Why or why not? How do you think Ji-li's identity is being influenced by the context of the Cultural Revolution?

For chapter 5, "Graduation," pp. 72–79

On page 73, Ji-li says, "I kept away from the Red Successors, from the rest of my classmates, from everyone." Why do you think Ji-li isolates herself? At the same time, she also participates in the isolation of Teacher Gu, a teacher she once admired. ("For nearly a month I had tried to avoid her," admits Ji-li on page 74.) Why do you think she participates in isolating Teacher Gu? Compare this situation to other examples in history, your own life, or in other stories where people have been isolated. What is the same? What is different? Is isolation ever an effective or appropriate response to a problem? Why or why not?

In this chapter, we learn that the way students are being assigned to schools has changed. Before the Cultural Revolution, students were assigned to schools based on grades and teacher recommendations, with the students with the highest academic achievement being assigned to the most prestigious schools. In the fall of 1966, students are being assigned to schools based on where they live. Which school assignment system do you think is most fair? Why? Many revolutionaries thought it was unfair to assign students to the best schools solely based on grades and teacher recommendations. Why do you think they believed this? What did they think was the relationship between class privilege and academic achievement? Do you think any of their arguments are relevant today?

On page 79, Ji-li writes, "I knew that many of my favorite books . . . would be sorted away forever, declared poison under the new standards." Why do you think that the Chinese authorities in charge of the Cultural Revolution wanted to burn certain books? Leaders throughout history have declared certain books to be dangerous and have taken actions to ban books. What does burning or banning books reveal about a society? What can get a book labeled as dangerous? Is there ever an appropriate time to ban a book? If so, when? German writer Heinrich Heine is famous for saying, "Where they burn books, they will ultimately also burn people." How does your understanding of history support or refute this statement?

For chapter 6, "The Sound of Drums and Gongs," pp. 80–99

How do characters react to "the sound of drums and gongs"? How might you explain the different responses to these searches? What was the role of the police or government authorities in the searches? Who could the victims of the searches turn to for protection? What can be done in a society when a government perpetuates violence against its own citizens?

Do you think the searches violated the human rights of the Chinese citizens? Why or why not? Under what conditions, if any, is it appropriate for a government or those working on behalf of the government to search a private home or business?

In this chapter, the Jiang family decides to fire Song Po-po. Compare the attitudes of different characters toward this decision. What does Song Po-po think of this decision? Ji-li? Ji-li's grandmother? Who might consider this a good decision? Who might say it was a bad decision? After taking different perspectives into account, do you agree with the decision made by Ji-li's parents to fire Song Po-po? Explain your answer.

At the end of this chapter, how do you think Ji-li feels about the Cultural Revolution?

USING DOCUMENTS: RED GUARDS

Background

The first Red Guard organization was formed by students at a prestigious middle school in Beijing. These students were critical of the "bourgeois" tendencies of their school administration. Though they were denounced as radicals by the school, Chairman Mao gave their group political legitimacy by publicizing its manifesto on the national radio and in the *People's Daily* newspaper. Soon Red Guard groups were forming throughout China, although they never had any central coordination or headquarters. In August 1966, Chairman Mao invited the Red Guards to Beijing and wore their signature red armband as a symbol of his support. Chairman Mao directed the Red Guards to destroy the Four Olds (tradition, culture, customs, and habits). The campaign began with the destruction of structures such as temples and Western-influenced buildings or shops, and big-character posters with sayings from Chairman Mao were plastered all over the cities. Soon the attacks were transferred to people, including intellectuals, members of "black category" families, and, finally, officials within the party suspected of counterrevolutionary activity. By October 1966, an official report noted the arrest of 22,000 "counterrevolutionaries" by Red Guards. In an effort to calm increasing violence committed by Red Guards, including bloody clashes between Red Guard factions, schools that had been closed in 1966 reopened in 1968. Rather than destroy the Four Olds, urban youth were encouraged to move to the countryside to work in agricultural production and learn from the peasants.[8]

- **Document 7:** *"A Little Red Solider," a poem from* Little Green: Growing Up During the Cultural Revolution

In the poem "A Little Red Soldier," Chun Yu uses the symbol of the red scarf to represent the loyal devotion many Chinese youth felt to their country, to the Cultural Revolution, and to Chairman Mao.

- **Document 8:** *"We Are Chairman Mao's Red Guards" and "Red Guards Battle Song," revolutionary songs (1968)*

Many songs were written to express support for the Cultural Revolution and for Mao Zedong. Young people were required to sing these songs in school, and they were also broadcast throughout China. These popular songs glorified the important role Red Guards were to play in the revolution and exemplify the messages Chinese youth received about their close relationship to Chairman Mao. The Morning Sun website (*www.morningsun.org*) provides an audio file of "We Are Chairman Mao's Red Guards," as performed by the Propaganda Team of the Political Department of China's People's Liberation Army. The Morning Sun website also posts the article "How the 'Red Guards Battle Song' Was Born," in which Red Guards from the Central Conservatory of Music explain the meaning of this song.

- **Document 9:** *"Hold high the great red banner of Mao Zedong Thought," poster (1966)*

The Chinese text on this poster reads, "Hold high the great red banner of Mao Zedong Thought to wage the Great Proletarian Cultural Revolution to the end. Revolution is no crime, to rebel is justified." Through their facial and body gestures, the four Red Guards in the foreground demonstrate the confidence and determination Chinese youth were supposed to feel in relation to the revolution. You can see that they are leading hundreds of other Red Guards who are marching behind them.

- **Document 10:** *"Red Guards reading from Mao's Red Book at Tiananmen Square," photograph (1966)*

This photograph shows a group of junior high girls, similar in age to Ji-li Jiang, who have traveled to Beijing to attend one of the many rallies organized for Red Guards from around the country.

- **Document 11:** *"Red Guards conduct a raid" (1966), an excerpt from* Life and Death in Shanghai *by Nien Chang*

In her memoir, London-educated Nien Chang, the widow of a Nationalist official and an employee of Shell Oil, describes what it was like to have her house ransacked by Red Guards in 1966.

We have selected the above poetry, images, and songs as a way to help students appreciate what life might have been like for Chinese youth who belonged to the Red Guards, and for those, like Ji-li Jiang, who were denied membership in this group. To help students explore all of these documents, the materials could be arranged around the room in stations, or you could use the *jigsaw teaching strategy*. After studying these documents, students can answer the question, "Who were the Red Guards?" They could write up their answer as an entry in an online encyclopedia, or as a newspaper article about Red Guards.

These documents also reveal the messages the Chinese youth were being sent about the proper ways to think and act. You can have students interpret these artifacts like anthropologists, noting what the materials say about Chinese youth culture at that time. Based on their careful study of these documents, students can create a list of the "Top Ten Ways Chinese Youth Were Told to Think and Act During the Cultural Revolution." This activity provides an opportunity for students to reflect on the influence of culture on their own ideas and behaviors. They can discuss questions such as these: How do music, images, movies, television, and other forms of culture influence the way young people think and act today? How can popular culture help create or reinforce in-groups and out-groups? How can popular culture break down barriers between groups? Students can even create their own "Top Ten" lists that reflect the messages they think youth today are sent about how to think and act.

EXTENSIONS

1. **The Bear that Wasn't:** Throughout this memoir, Ji-li is confused about her own identity. On the one hand, she believes she is a "model student" and a loyal Chinese citizen. On the other hand, she receives messages from some of her peers suggesting that she is a disloyal "black whelp" in need of "remolding." What is she supposed to believe about her own identity? How do the perceptions of others shape the way we think of ourselves? Frank Tashlin's illustrated short story *The Bear that Wasn't* can help students appreciate the internal conflict Ji-li faces as she struggles with her own identity. In Tashlin's allegory, a bear wakes up after a long hibernation to a changed world. In this world, everyone believes he is a man, not a bear. The bear's confidence in his identity as a bear decreases as he receives consistent messages that he is a man, much like how Ji-li's confidence in her own sense of self changes as she receives messages that she is a rightist who can never be a full member of the revolution. *The Bear that Wasn't* is included in Chapter 1 of the resource book, *Facing History and Ourselves: Holocaust and Human Behavior*, on pages 7–9. This chapter can be downloaded from our website: *www.facinghistory.org/resources/hhb*. Members of the Facing History network can borrow class sets of this book from our library.

2. **Point-of-view writing:** During the Cultural Revolution, house searches were a prominent tool used to rally the masses, silence resistance, promote obedience, and gather information. In this section of the memoir, Ji-li describes a house search from the perspective of a bystander—someone who witnesses the event but does not directly participate in it. To help students more deeply understand house searches, you might ask them to write about a search from the perspective of a different character, such as Six-Fingers or Mr. Rong. Before beginning this exercise, students might record their

own thoughts about house searches. Then, after students share the house-search stories they wrote, they can discuss how listening to stories about searches from different perspectives alters the way they understand this event. This activity helps students think about the concept of point of view in both literature and history. As they continue reading *Red Scarf Girl*, students can return to questions about point of view, such as:

- What is Ji-li's perspective on the Cultural Revolution? How does her identity influence her recounting of this historical event?

- How might your understanding of the Cultural Revolution be different if you read a memoir written by a different character in this story?

3. **The right to privacy:** How should society balance individuals' right to privacy and a nation's security concerns? Under what conditions, if any, is it appropriate for a government official to search the private property of citizens? Reading about house searches during the Cultural Revolution raises these questions. To help students think about issues of privacy and national security more broadly, you might consider one of the following activities:

- Groups of students can identify scenarios in which they think it is appropriate for the government to conduct searches of private property and conditions when it is inappropriate for the government to conduct searches of private property. Using this information as a guide, the class as a whole can create a list of criteria that governments should use when deciding whether or not a search is fair and appropriate.

- Students can conduct research on privacy laws in their nation. The FindLaw website (*www.findlaw.com*) is an excellent source for information about privacy rights in the United States, including information on the Fourth Amendment, search and seizure, and electronic surveillance. Based on research and personal opinion, students can debate the appropriateness and fairness of government-sponsored house searches.

---

[1] David Ashley, *Mao's Children in the New China: Voices From the Red Guard Generation*, ed. Yarong Jiang (Routledge, 2000), 13.

[2] Ibid., 165.

[3] Ibid., 25.

[4] Ibid., 21.

[5] Ibid., 21.

[6] Xing Lu, *Rhetoric of the Chinese Cultural Revolution: The Impact of Chinese Thought, Culture, and Communication* (University of South Carolina Press, 2004), 55.

[7] Lu, *Rhetoric of the Chinese Cultural Revolution*, 55.

[8] Thomas P. Bernstein, *Up to the Mountains and Down to the Villages: The Transfer of Youth from Urban to Rural China* (Yale University Press, 1977).

DOCUMENT 7

"A Little Red Soldier," a poem from *Little Green: Growing Up During the Cultural Revolution* [1]

When I turned eight,

I was a Little Red Soldier

in the Young Pioneers group

like almost everyone else in the school.

Each of us had a little red scarf,

which we were told was

a corner of the five-star red flag of the country,

dyed red by the revolutionary **martyrs'** blood.

We wore our scarves to school every day.

GLOSSARY

martyrs: people who would rather die that give up the principle or cause that they believe in

DOCUMENT 8

"We Are Chairman Mao's Red Guards" and "Red Guards Battle Song," revolutionary songs (1968)

The two songs in this document were written by Red Guards during the Cultural Revolution. Young people sang them in school and at rallies, and they were played over the radio throughout China.

"We Are Chairman Mao's Red Guards"[2]

Red Guards, Red Guards,

Burning with revolutionary zeal,

Tested by the storm of class struggle,

Tempered for battle our hearts are red,

Standing firm, direction clear,

*Our **vigor** for revolution strong,*

We follow the party with full devotion,

We are Chairman Mao's Red Guards

Red Guards, Red Guards,

*We want to be the **successors** to Communism.*

The revolutionary red banner passes on from generation to generation,

We want to carry on the glorious tradition.

*Loving the country, loving the People, loving the **Collective**,*
* loving to work.*

Connecting with the workers and the peasants,

We are Chairman Mao's Red Guards.

"Red Guards Battle Song"[3]

We are Chairman Mao's Red Guards,

We steel our red hearts in great winds and waves.

We arm ourselves with Mao Tse–Tung's thought

To sweep away all pests.

We are Chairman Mao's Red Guards,

Absolutely firm in our **proletarian** stand,

Marching on the revolutionary road of our **forbears**,

We shoulder the heavy task of our age.

We are Chairman Mao's Red Guards,

Vanguards of the cultural revolution.

We unite with the masses and together plunge into the battle

To wipe out all monsters and demons.

[**Refrain**] Dare to criticize and **repudiate**, dare to struggle,

Never stop making revolutionary rebellion.

We will smash the old world

And keep our revolutionary state red for ten thousand generations!

GLOSSARY

collective: a community organized to live and work together

forbears: ancestors

proletarian: related to the working class

refrain: the chorus of a song

repudiate: to criticize and reject something for not being true or right

successors: followers; people who continue a tradition

vanguards: leaders of a movement

vigor: strength and force to accomplish a certain goal

"Hold high the great red banner of Mao Zedong Thought," poster (1966)

The Chinese text on this poster reads "Hold high the great red banner of Mao Zedong Thought to wage the Great Proletarian Cultural Revolution to the end. Revolution is no crime, to rebel is justified."

DOCUMENT 10

"Red Guards reading from Mao's Red Book at Tiananmen Square," photograph (1966)

Red Guards stand in front of an image of Chairman Mao while reading from *The Collected Quotations of Chairman Mao Zedong*, also known as Mao's *Little Red Book*.

DOCUMENT 11

"Red Guards conduct a raid" (1966), an excerpt from *Life and Death in Shanghai* by Nien Chang [4]

From the direction of the street, faint at first but growing louder, came the sound of a heavy motor vehicle slowly approaching. I listened and waited for it to speed up and pass the house. But it slowed down, and the motor was cut off. I knew my neighbor on the left was also expecting the Red Guards. Dropping the book on my lap and sitting up tensely, I listened, wondering which house was to be the target.

*Suddenly the doorbell began to ring **incessantly**. At the same time, there was furious pounding of many fists on my front gate, accompanied by the confused sound of hysterical voices shouting slogans. The **cacophony** told me that the time of waiting was over and that I must face the threat of the Red Guards and the destruction of my home. . . . The Red Guards pushed open the front door and entered the house. There were thirty or forty senior high students, aged between fifteen and twenty, led by two men and one woman much older. Although they all wore the armband of the Red Guard, I thought the three older people were the teachers who generally accompanied the Red Guards. . . .*

*The leading Red Guard, a gangling youth with angry eyes, stepped forward and said to me, "We are the Red Guards. We have come to take revolutionary action against you!" Though I knew it was futile, I held up the copy of the Constitution and said calmly, "It's against the Constitution of the People's Republic of China to enter a private house without a search warrant." The young man snatched the document out of my hand and threw it on the floor. With his eyes blazing, he said, "The Constitution is abolished. It was a document written by the **Revisionists** within the Communist Party. We recognize only the teachings of our Great Leader Chairman Mao.". . .*

*Another young man used a stick to smash the mirror hanging over the blackwood chest facing the front door . . . I sat down by the dining table and looked around the room. It was strange to realize that after this night I would never see it again as it was. . . I listened to the laughter of the Red Guards overheard. They seemed so blissfully happy in their work of destruction because they were sure they were doing something to satisfy their God, Mao Zedong. Their behavior was the result of their upbringing in Communist China. The propaganda they had absorbed **precluded** their having a free will of their own. . . . Mounting the stairs, I was astonished to see several Red Guards taking pieces of my porcelain collection out of their padded boxes. One young man had arranged a set of four **Kangzi** wine cups in a row on the floor and was stepping on them. I was just in time to hear the crunch of the delicate porcelain under the sole of his shoe. The sound pierced my heart. . .*

*I looked at what had happened to my things, hopelessly but **indifferently**. They belonged to a period of my life that had abruptly ended when the Red Guards entered my house. Though I could not see into the future, I refused to look back. I supposed the Red Guards had enjoyed themselves. Is it not true that we all possess some destructive tendencies in our nature? The **veneer** of civilization is very thin. Underneath lurks the animal in each of us. If I were young and had had a working–class background, if I had been brought up to worship Mao and taught to believe him **infallible**, would I not have behaved exactly as the Red Guards had done?*

GLOSSARY

cacophony: loud noises that are harsh and unpleasant

incessantly: an action that goes on and on for a long period of time

indifferently: unemotionally

infallible: incapable of making mistakes

Kangzi: antique, coming from the time of the Kangzi emperor (1654–1722)

precluded: to make something unlikely or impossible

Revisionists: those who are trying to change communism to make it more like the old system (pre-1949)

veneer: the top layer of something

---

[1] Chun Yu, *Little Green: Growing Up During the Chinese Cultural Revolution* (Simon and Schuster Books for Young Readers, 2005), 68.

[2] "Listen to the Radio," *Morning Sun* website, *http://www.morningsun.org/multimedia /we_are_red_guards.html* (accessed June 9, 2009).

[3] "Smash the Old World!" *Morning Sun* website, *http://www.morningsun.org/smash /cr_3_1968.html* (accessed June 9, 2009).

[4] Nien Cheng, *Life and Death in Shanghai* (Penguin Books, 1988), excerpts 70–73, 78–79.

PART 3: OBEDIENCE TO THE REVOLUTION

Includes chapters "The Propaganda Wall" (pp. 100–117),
"A Search in Passing" (pp. 118–139), and "Fate" (pp. 140–155)

OVERVIEW

Like other powerful leaders in history, Chairman Mao effectively mobilized the national youth to serve his political agenda. Mao, recognizing the importance of youth in shaping the future of China, told a group of students, "The world is yours, as well as ours, but in the last analysis it is yours. You young people, full of vigor and vitality, are in the bloom of life, like the sun at eight or nine in the morning. Our hope is placed on you. . ."[1] The leaders of the Cultural Revolution employed many strategies to encourage youth to participate in this movement. For example, between August and November of 1966, the Communist Party organized Red Guard rallies in Beijing's Tiananmen Square. Instead of attending school, students were traveling across China to "spread revolution." Free train fare made it possible for millions of youth to visit Beijing and other revolutionary centers. In chapter 7, Ji-li stands in a packed auditorium with her peers to hear Jia Hong-yu recount her experience of seeing Mao at a Red Guard rally in Beijing. Just hearing about the rally makes the crowd of students cry and weep before they rise and shout, "Long live Chairman Mao! Long live Chairman Mao!" The rallies, slogans, and special uniforms helped youth feel like they belonged to something larger than themselves. As long as you were from a "red" class background, fitting in was as simple as chanting the right song and having the proper armband.

In addition to organizing rallies, the leaders of the Cultural Revolution attracted the attention of Chinese youth, and the Chinese public in general, by the effective use of propaganda—information spread for the purpose of influencing opinions—often for or against a specific political agenda. The leaders of the Cultural Revolution used posters, newspapers, songs, theater, cinema, stories, and other media to glorify the Communist Party and Chairman Mao and to create distinctions between red and black groups. At the beginning of chapter 7, Ji-li describes how party messages were posted on "propaganda walls" in every neighborhood. During rituals such as Morning Repentance and Evening Report, people in the Five Black Categories had to make confessions and to praise Mao by chanting party slogans. These public demonstrations served as a constant reminder that belonging to the wrong group carried serious consequences.

Morning Repentance and Evening Report are just one example of how the leaders of the Cultural Revolution used fear and humiliation to thwart resistance to their campaigns. Ji-li shares how "the Neighborhood Dictatorship Group seemed to be everywhere" (p. 103), and in these chapters we read about the increasing prevalence of house searches, arrests, and struggle sessions. Knowing that they are being watched and that anyone might be the next target engenders fear in the Jiang household and in households throughout China, particularly in urban areas, where most of the Red Guard activity was taking place. "Every time I hear drums and gongs, I'm afraid that they're coming to our house," laments Ji-li's worried grandmother (p. 120). Between the omnipresent propaganda and the visible consequences for being labeled a Black Category, it is not surprising that Ji-li reports, "The Neighborhood Dictatorship Group and the Black Categories were all we could think of" (p. 102).

One of the consequences of the propaganda and fear tactics employed by the leaders of the Cultural Revolution was to perpetuate harmful stereotypes that "turned neighbor against neighbor." Anyone with the wrong class background was believed to be against the revolution and, therefore, a potential threat to society. On page 142, we read about how a son refused to help his own mother who was labeled as a Black Category. Ji-li also describes examples of how students turn against their teachers, such as An Yi's mother, and how junior officers turned against their superiors, like Xiao-cheng's father. According to Hao Jiang Tian, who grew up during the Cultural Revolution,

> Suspicions spread through the [neighborhood] like bad smells. I sensed them, though I was still too young to understand much of what they meant. . . . No one wanted to have a so-called counterrevolutionary in their midst. . . . And, human relationships being what they are, people also found a potent tool to get revenge on their enemies, those with whom they were competing for higher rank and privilege—or others whom they wanted to bring down.[2]

As Hao Jiang Tian explains, the system of labeling and persecution encouraged during the Cultural Revolution created an environment that pitted neighbor against neighbor. And, while the Cultural Revolution propaganda promoted supreme loyalty to Chairman Mao, the culture of distrust created during the movement encouraged some people to focus only on self-preservation.

Studying the Cultural Revolution provides insights into what can happen when a government creates conditions where neighbors no longer trust each other. By creating a culture where individuals were rewarded for placing Chairman Mao and the Communist Party above their friends, colleagues, and families, the leaders of the Cultural Revolution made it possible for ordinary people, especially youth, to alienate and harm their fellow citizens. According to Professor Stanley Rosen, "With the coming of the Cultural Revolution they [Chinese citizens born in the late 1940s and early 1950s] transferred their complete devotion to Chairman Mao, competing to be the most loyal followers of the Chairman. Under these conditions they could commit the most violent crimes with the purest hearts."[3] Today, in our schools and across the globe, we can find examples of when individuals, and sometimes even our own students, experience stereotyping, fear, and humiliation. They might be victims, bystanders, or even perpetrators of these acts. An understanding of the conditions that gave rise to distrust and intolerance during the Cultural Revolution can make students more aware of how to prevent or stand up to these conditions in their own communities.

ESSENTIAL QUESTIONS

What is propaganda? How can media be used to control and influence public opinion? What other tools and strategies can governments employ to influence the beliefs and behaviors of its citizens?

What is a stereotype? What encourages stereotypes? What prevents or breaks down stereotypes? How does stereotyping individuals lead to prejudice and discrimination?

What conditions give rise to distrust and intolerance among members of a community?

What helps define the universe of responsibility of a nation, group, or individual? What are the consequences for individuals and groups who are considered outside of a community's universe of responsibility?

SUGGESTED ACTIVITIES

DISCUSSIONS AND JOURNAL WRITING

For chapter 7, "The Propaganda Wall" (pp. 100–117)

What messages are the Communist Party and Red Guards sending to Chinese youth during the Cultural Revolution? How? What messages do you think are being sent to youth today? Compare these messages and how they are disseminated. What are the similarities and differences between the use of media and propaganda during the Cultural Revolution and the use of media and propaganda in society today?

On page 103, Ji-li describes some of the responsibilities of the Neighborhood Dictatorship Group. What do you think was the purpose of the Neighborhood Dictatorship Group? What role did this group play in strengthening and/or weakening the community? Under what conditions can civil associations (organized groups of citizens) strengthen a community?

On page 104, Jia Hong-yu explains her decision to travel to Beijing to see Chairman Mao, despite the objections of her father and her mother's illness. "But how can we put personal matters ahead of the revolution?" she asks the students in the auditorium. What do you think is happening in China that might be influencing young people to care more about Chairman Mao and the revolution than they care about their own family or friends? What do you think might be influencing the civic attitude—feelings about government and politics—of youth today?

Chairman Mao did not make many public appearances. Thus, his decision to appear at a Red Guard rally in Beijing was very significant. Mao also openly supported the Red Guards in speeches he gave throughout 1966. Why do you think Mao supported the Red Guards? Why do leaders often involve youth in social change movements? What are the benefits of youth participation in social change movements? What challenges might arise from youth involvement?

Jia Hong-yu describes how the Red Guards were cramped, tired, hungry, and hot as they waited for Mao in Tiananmen Square (pages 106–107). Throughout history, young activists like Jia Hong-yu have eagerly joined social change movements, despite uncomfortable conditions. For example, in 1965, young people walked over 200 miles with thousands of others to protest voter discrimination in the United States. What do you think encourages young people to get involved in social change movements? Why might some young people be attracted to joining revolutionary causes?

For chapter 8, "A Search in Passing" (pp. 118–139)

On page 121, Ji-li says, "She doesn't seem like a landlord's wife," referring to her own grandmother. What allows Ji-li to hold misgivings about the stereotype of the landlord's wife generated by government propaganda? What does this moment reveal about stereotypes in general?

On page 126, Ji-li recalls, "I wondered what I would be doing if I had been born into a red family instead of a black one." Help Ji-li answer this question. How might her experiences and beliefs be different if she were a member of a different family? To what extent do you think family shapes personal identity? What else influences our beliefs and actions?

In this section, Ji-yong's army cap is stolen, and Ji-li's stamp collection is confiscated by the Red Guards. How do each of these characters react when their cherished possessions are taken from them? What do their reactions reveal about these characters? Identify one of your most cherished possessions. What does this object say about you? How would you react if it were taken from you?

After her house is searched, Ji-li wonders, "Wasn't home a private place? A place where the family could feel secure?" How would you answer Ji-li's questions? What does it mean to feel secure? What is the relationship between security and privacy? Is it possible to feel secure without the right to privacy?

For chapter 9, "Fate" (pp. 140–155)

At the beginning of this chapter, Ji-li describes watching Shan-shan walk by his mother, who had just fallen and was struggling to get up. Who is the victim in this situation? The bystander? The perpetrator? The upstander? What role does Ji-li play?

On page 146, Ji-li declares, "When I looked around me, fate seemed to be the only explanation for what was happening." What do you think she means by this statement? What could be other explanations, besides fate, to explain what was happening in China at that time?

Fear and humiliation were two tools used by the Red Guards during the Cultural Revolution. Identify moments from this chapter when these tactics were used. What impact might fear and humiliation have on the victims? On those who witness these acts (the bystanders)? How might this kind of bullying behavior impact the perpetrators of these acts? Given the circumstances during the Cultural Revolution, to what extent was it possible to resist being publicly humiliated?

Today, in our schools and across the globe, we can find examples when individuals experience stereotyping, fear, and humiliation. What can we do to help individuals prevent or stand up to stereotyping and discrimination?

During the Cultural Revolution, what aspects of Chinese society were helping to unite people? What aspects of Chinese society were dividing people? Overall, do you think the Cultural Revolution was a movement aimed more at bringing people together or creating divisions? Explain your answer.

USING DOCUMENTS: PROPAGANDA POSTERS

Background

During the Cultural Revolution, propaganda posters were distributed throughout the country. We have selected three propaganda posters for students to analyze, including the poster "Mao Ze-dong on His Way to Anyuan," referenced on page 101 of *Red Scarf Girl*. "Mao Ze-dong on His Way to Anyuan," one of the most important paintings of the Cultural Revolution period, depicts a 27-year-old Mao on his way to lead a coal miners' strike in 1922. Hundreds of millions of copies of the painting were printed as posters, under the encouragement of Jiang Qing, Mao's wife and one of the leaders of the Cultural Revolution. The painting was showcased in a special exhibition at China's Museum of the Revolution in 1967 that was part of a deliberate campaign to discredit Liu Shaoqi, president of the People's Republic of China from 1959 until his imprisonment as a counterrevolutionary in 1968. Though he was once a close colleague of Mao's, after the failures of the Great Leap Forward* Mao concluded that Liu Shaoqi's policies were leading China away from socialism and, therefore, that Liu was a threat to his (Mao's) power. The painting suggests that Mao alone deserves credit for the achievements of the labor movement in Anyuan, as opposed to early narratives that included Liu Shaoqi as key to the success of the miners' strike.[4]

"Mao Ze-dong on His Way to Anyuan" was planned by a group of students in Beijing and painted by Liu Chunhua, a Red Guard member. Liu explains how the painting was explicitly designed to glorify Chairman Mao:

> *To put him in a focal position, we placed Chairman Mao in the forefront of the painting, advancing towards us like a rising sun bringing hope to the people. . . His head held high in the act of surveying the scene before him conveys his revolutionary spirit, dauntless before danger and violence, and courageous in struggle, and in "daring to win"; his clenched fist depicts his revolutionary will, scorning all sacrifice, his determination to surmount every difficulty to emancipate China and mankind, and it shows his confidence in victory. The old umbrella under his right arm demonstrates his hard–working style of traveling, in all weather over great distances, across the mountains and rivers, for the revolutionary cause [. . .] The hair grown long in a very busy life is blown by the autumn wind. His long plain gown, fluttering in the wind, is a harbinger of the approaching revolutionary storm [. . .] With the arrival of our great leader, blue skies appear over Anyuan. The hills, sky, trees, and clouds are the means used artistically to evoke a grand image of the red sun in our hearts. Riotous clouds are drifting swiftly past. They indicate that Chairman Mao is arriving in Anyuan at a critical point of sharp class struggle, and show, in contrast, how tranquil, confident, and firm Chairman Mao is at that moment [. . .][5]*

The success of propaganda in influencing the minds and hearts of many Chinese, especially Chinese youth, demonstrates the dangers that can befall a society whose citizens are not able to make informed judgments about the media around them. By

---

*In 1958, Chairman Mao implemented a series of policies aimed at modernizing China's economy. This five-year initiative was called the Great Leap Forward.

helping students develop the ability to answer questions about the intended purpose of the text, the message being expressed, and the validity of the information, we nurture their growth as responsible citizens.

- **Document 12:** *"Mao Ze-dong on His Way to Anyuan"* (1968)

- **Document 13:** *"Scatter the old world, build a new world"* (1967)

- **Document 14:** *"Chairman Mao will be with us forever"* (1968)

There are many ways in which these propaganda posters can be used to help students develop a deeper understanding of propaganda and the Cultural Revolution. To help students interpret these images, refer to the teaching strategy *developing media literacy: analyzing propaganda and other images*. Small groups can analyze one poster and present their analysis to the class.* Alternatively, students could write an essay comparing two or three propaganda posters and explaining what the posters reveal about China during the Cultural Revolution. Interpreting Chinese propaganda posters not only teaches students about the context of the Cultural Revolution but also helps students recognize visual techniques used to express a message. Most of the propaganda posters created during the Cultural Revolution contained famous quotations from Chairman Mao, and artists used composition, color, and imagery to help communicate his ideas. After studying the techniques used by Chinese artists, students can select a quotation that is meaningful to them (or write their own) and then design their own propaganda posters to express this message.

One important point for students to take away from this exercise is that propaganda is designed to express an intended message to a particular audience. The effectiveness of the document depends on how the messenger (creator) was able to use words, pictures, color, and composition to communicate this message. After students interpret the meaning of these, it is important that they also evaluate them from an ethical standpoint. Just because a piece of propaganda is effective, that does not mean that the text is fair or ethical. Often effective propaganda, including propaganda disseminated during the Cultural Revolution, uses lies or misleading information to convey ideas. Should all propaganda be considered unethical, even propaganda aimed at causes we support? Many forms of media (i.e., advertising, political campaign speeches, public service announcements) are produced with the purpose of persuading public opinion and might be classified as propaganda. What criteria should we use to evaluate the ethical use of information? How might we distinguish between the use and the abuse of information? In the twenty-first century, when most of us have increasing access to a wide range of information, it is especially important for students to be equipped with the ability not only to comprehend ideas but also to evaluate this information from a moral and intellectual perspective.

---

* For additional propaganda posters, the website *chineseposters.net* organizes posters by programs implemented during the Cultural Revolution, such as the Seven May Cadre Schools and Up to the Mountains, Down to the Villages. Stefan Landsberger's Chinese Propaganda Poster Pages site (*www.iisg.nl/landsberger*) includes background information about the use of propaganda posters in China since 1937 and provides many examples of posters from the Cultural Revolution.

EXTENSIONS

1. Appreciating the complexity of decision-making: Facing History teachers often use the language of bystander, victim, perpetrator, and upstander to help students understand the roles played by individuals and groups during times of injustice or violence. After introducing these terms, you can assign a chapter to a pair of students and ask them to label the characters in that chapter as bystanders, victims, perpetrators, or upstanders. Pairs can share their responses with another pair that was assigned the same chapter. When debriefing this exercise, ask students if they think it is possible for someone to perform more than one role. For example, can someone be a bystander and a victim at the same time? Drawing from experiences in their own lives and their understanding of the Cultural Revolution and other histories, students can discuss the conditions that might encourage bystander and perpetrator behavior and the conditions that might encourage individuals to stand up to injustice. You might also have students repeat this activity but from the perspective of a Red Guard. For example, while Ji-li presents herself and her family as victims, a Red Guard might perceive the Jiang family as perpetrators. This exercise reveals how point of view shapes the way we judge the actions of groups and individuals. Just because the Red Guards perceived themselves as upstanders, however, does not mean that they were acting in ways to prevent injustice. Ultimately, students should come away from this activity with an appreciation for the complexity of decision-making and judgment, not with a sense of moral relativism.

2. Making connections: The issues raised in *Red Scarf Girl* can resonate with students on many levels. One way to help students recognize the universal themes in this text is by asking them to identify connections between an idea from *Red Scarf Girl* and something they have read in another text, something they have experienced, and something they know about society, past or present. See the ☑**TEACHING STRATEGIES** section for a description of the *text-to-text, text-to-self, text-to-world* teaching strategy.

---

[1] "Mao Zedong talk at a meeting with Chinese students and trainees in Moscow, November 17, 1957," *Quotations from Chairman Mao Tse-Tung* (Bantam, 1976), 165.

[2] Hao Jiang Tian, *Along the Roaring River: My Wild Ride from Mao to the Met* (John Wiley and Sons Inc., 2008), 31.

[3] Yarong Jiang and David Ashley, *Mao's Children in the New China* (Routledge, 2000), xv.

[4] Elizabeth J. Perry, "Reclaiming the Chinese Revolution," *The Journal of Asian Studies* 67:4 (2008), 1147–1164.

[5] "Chairman Mao goes to Anyuan," Chinese Posters website, *http://chineseposters.net/themes/mao-anyuan.php* (accessed June 4, 2009).

"Mao Ze–dong on His Way to Anyuan" (1968)

毛 主 席 去 安 源

一九二一年秋，我们伟大的导师毛主席去安源，亲自点燃了安源的革命烈火。

DOCUMENT 13

"Scatter the old world, build a new world" (1967)

PART 4: SHAPING THE YOUTH

Includes "Junior High School at Last" (pp. 156–172), "Locked Up" (pp. 173–190), and "An Educable Child" (pp. 191–205)

OVERVIEW

At the beginning of *Red Scarf Girl*, Ji-li was 12, and the Cultural Revolution had just started. Now Ji-li is 14. For over a year, Red Guards and the "masses" have been directed to follow the instructions outlined by the Central Committee of the Chinese Communist Party on August 8, 1966, in its "Decision Concerning the Great Proletarian Cultural Revolution" (also known as "The Sixteen Points"). (See the Using Documents section on page 84 for more information about the Sixteen Points.) With economic production down and chaos in the streets, in 1967, Chairman Mao asks the army to help restore order and decides to reopen schools to contain the Red Guards.

Chapter 10 begins with Ji-li starting junior high school after more than a year without any classes. Prior to the Cultural Revolution, she had dreamed of studying physics. Now she describes how her science teacher struggles to teach students about pigs and paddy fields. Her English classes are dominated by reciting Communist Party slogans. Ji-li's experience in school reflects how the Chinese education system had changed during the Cultural Revolution. Indeed, Point 10 of the Sixteen Points directive clearly expressed how education should serve the revolution:

> *In every kind of school we must apply thoroughly the policy advanced by Comrade Mao Tse-tung of education serving proletarian politics, and education being combined with productive labor, so as to enable those receiving an education to develop morally, intellectually, and physically, and to become laborers with socialist consciousness and culture.*[1]

Mao was not the only leader to appreciate the important role schools play in preparing youth to be members of society. One of Hitler's first acts as Chancellor of Germany was to appoint a Minister of Propaganda whom he put in charge of education. While it may seem that only totalitarian or communist governments believe schools serve an important role in preparing youth for their role in society, most democratic nations, including the United States, also declare that one of the purposes of public education is to prepare youth for their role as citizens.[2] The question is not whether schools are involved with the task of civic education but, rather, "What kind of citizen does a particular type of schooling prepare students to become?"

Reading about Ji-li's experience in school can help us think more deeply about the connection between schooling and citizenship, including questions such as "How might schooling in a dictatorship be different from schooling in a democracy?" and "What does a society's education system reveal about its values?" The leaders of the Cultural Revolution reformed the education system to produce students who would follow Chairman Mao without question. As one former Red Guard explained, "All our lives we were brought up to believe that the Party was always right and, of course, Chairman Mao was the Party. . . However, there's something this kind of education gave me that I'll always hate. I was conditioned to blindly follow the leadership and never to think for myself."[3] On the other hand, another former Red Guard disagrees with this statement, declaring, "Many people now like to claim that during the Cultural Revolution, we were victims of indoctrination. Well, if we were 'victims' it was our choice. The Red Guards behaved as they did, not because they had been 'tricked' into being idealists, but because they'd figured out how to best respond to their environment. What's so unusual about that?"[4]

Regardless of whether young people were blindly following Mao's teachings or choosing to do so, the effect was more or less the same: youth were conditioned to value Chairman Mao, and the Party, above everything else. In his memoir *Along the Roaring River*, Hao Jiang Tian explains this zealous loyalty to Mao as follows:

> *Children were so empowered in those days that we could turn in our parents or someone else's in criticism sessions in school. As the oft-repeated saying went, "Mother is close, father is close, but neither is as close as Chairman Mao." Our sole allegiance was supposed to be to you-know-who. If you didn't have a good family background, you'd have to say, "I was born in a black family. I don't want to be their children. I will help them to clean their minds."*[5]

Hao Jiang Tian's experience is echoed throughout *Red Scarf Girl*. For example, on page 190, the foreman tells Ji-li, "You are a child of Chairman Mao. You can choose your own destiny: You can make a clean break with your parents and follow Chairman Mao, and have a bright future; or you can follow your parents, and then . . . you will not come to a good end." And, in chapter 12, we learn how Ji-li's classmate, Chang Hong, places the revolution and Mao at the center of her universe of responsibility, saying, "[W]e can't allow personal matters to interfere with revolutionary duties" (p. 205).

Comparing the decisions made by different characters in *Red Scarf Girl* can help us think more deeply about the factors that might encourage some people to conform to society's norms, or blindly follow a leader, while others choose to resist authority and peer pressure. Schooling and propaganda influence people in different ways. While many Chinese youth, like the characters Shan-shan and Chang Hong, decided to put Mao and the revolution above their families, Ji-li still feels obligated to protect the members of her family. Her decision not to criticize her father might be interpreted as an act of resistance within the political context of the Cultural Revolution. Ultimately, exploring the choices made by characters in this memoir raises important questions about the relationship between the individual and society.

ESSENTIAL QUESTIONS

Under what conditions will many people, especially young people, blindly follow and obey a leader? Under these same conditions, why do some people decide not to obey authority?

What is the role of schools in preparing young people for their role as citizens? What does a society's education system reveal about its values and culture?

What does it mean to be an upstander? What do you think encourages and inspires people to stand up to injustice and help people in need? What do you think prevents or discourages upstander behavior?

What helps to define the universe of responsibility of a nation, group, or individual? To whom do you feel most responsible? Why? What are the consequences for individuals and groups who are considered outside of a community's universe of responsibility?

SUGGESTED ACTIVITIES

DISCUSSIONS AND JOURNAL WRITING

For chapter 10, "Junior High School at Last" (pp. 156–172)

On pages 156–160, Ji-li describes her first day in her new junior high school. (Note: In China, junior high is equivalent to secondary school in other countries.) Compare the events and feelings she experienced on her first day at Xin-zha Junior High School to your first day at a new school. Does anything she describes about her day feel familiar to you? What was different? Do you strongly agree, agree, disagree, or strongly disagree with the following statement: "My first day at a new school was very similar to Ji-li's first day at Xin-zha Junior High School"? Explain your answer.

When Ji-li forgets her *Little Red Book*, she worries about being criticized in front of the whole school. Then her classmate Sun Lin-lin hands Ji-li the cover of her *Little Red Book* to hold up. After looking "gratefully" at her "rescuer," Ji-li thinks, "If I had been in her position . . . I would never even have noticed the problem, let alone come up with such a quick solution" (p. 168). How would you explain Sun Lin-lin's behavior? What encourages people to notice when others need help? After recognizing a problem, what encourages people to act in ways to improve the situation? To what extent can schools teach students the habits of empathy and social responsibility? Where else do young people develop these habits of caring and action?

At the end of this chapter, Ji-li is asked to join the propaganda group for the school newspaper. This is considered an honor. How does her reaction to being asked to join the propaganda group compare to her reaction to being asked to audition for the Central Liberation Army Arts Academy (from chapter 1)? What happened in the past 18 months that might explain her different responses to being singled out? What impact might distinguishing a few students have on the larger group? What impact might it have on those particular students who are being singled out? Under what conditions do you think it is appropriate to single out particular students in school? Does your answer change if you consider distinguishing students for positive achievements as opposed to singling out students for negative behavior?

For chapter 11, "Locked Up" (pp. 173–190)

In this chapter, Ji-li describes the Communist Party's stance on confessions. What was the purpose of these confessions?

On page 177, Ji-li's father explains how he is being pressured to confess anti-Party actions he has not committed. On the following pages, his family discusses reasons for and against confessing. Which argument do you find most convincing? What might be gained by confessing? What might be lost? What advice would you give to Ji-li's father?

How does the Jiang family resist the authorities in the Communist Party? What are the consequences of their resistance? Do you think their actions to disobey the government were justified? Why or why not?

On page 190, the foreman of the scene shop says to Ji-li, "You are different from your parents. You were born and raised in New China. You are a child of Chairman Mao. You can choose your own destiny: You can make a clean break with your parents and follow Chairman Mao, and have a bright future; or you can follow your parents, and then . . . you will not come to a good end." What message is being sent to Ji-li about how she should define her universe of responsibility? What dilemma does she face? If she asked you for advice after leaving the foreman's office, what would you say?

In your community, what messages are expressed about how youth should define their universe of responsibility? To whom should young people today feel a sense of responsibility? How do these messages compare to the messages being sent to youth during the Cultural Revolution in China?

For chapter 12, "An Educable Child" (pp. 191–205)

On page 195, the leader of the school Revolutionary Committee, Chairman Jin, announces, "In order to support the Cultural Revolution and promote class struggle, our school's Red Guard Committee has decided to make a Class Education Exhibit to expose the class enemies' evil and remind us of the misery of the old society and our happiness today." What does the Class Education Exhibit the students create reveal about the values and beliefs of Chinese society during the Cultural Revolution? If you and your peers were asked to create a Class Education Exhibit to showcase the values of your society, what might the exhibit include?

Based on what you know about Ji-li's school experiences, what do the leaders of the Cultural Revolution believe is the purpose of schooling? Based on your experience as a student, how do you think your community defines the purpose of schooling? What do you think is the purpose of school? What is the relationship between school and citizenship?

On page 205, Ji-li asks Chang Hong why she has decided to be a Red Guard and participate in revolutionary activities that take her outside the home, even though she has a sick brother who depends on her. "[W]e can't allow personal matters to interfere with revolutionary duties," she explains. Why might Chang Hong have felt this way? What did Cultural Revolution propaganda express was the ideal relationship between the individual and the state? What are the implications for a society if individuals prioritize national matters above "personal matters"? What do you think should be the relationship between the individual and the state?

USING DOCUMENTS: GOVERNMENT-ISSUED DOCUMENTS

• **Document 15:** *Selected "Quotations from Chairman Mao Zedong," The Little Red Book*

In 1964, the Political Department of the People's Liberation Army (PLA) published the first edition of *Quotations from Chairman Mao Zedong*. "Study Chairman Mao's writings, follow his teachings, and act according to his instructions," declared Lin Biao, a general in the PLA and one of the leaders of the Communist Party.[6] In the introduction to *Quotations from Chairman Mao Zedong*, which was often called "The Precious Little Red Book" or "The Little Red Book" because of its bright red plastic cover, Lin goes on to explain how memorizing Mao's quotations could help all Chinese—"workers, peasants, and soldiers"—build China "into a great socialist state." He wrote:

> *In order really to master Mao Tse-tung's thought, it is essential to study many of Chairman Mao's basic concepts over and over again, and it is best to memorize important statements and study and apply them repeatedly. . . . We have compiled* Quotations from Chairman Mao Tse-tung *in order to help the broad masses learn Mao Tse-tung's thought more effectively. In organizing their study, units should select passages that are relevant to the situation, their tasks, the current thinking of their personnel, and the state of their work. . . . Once Mao Tse-tung's thought is grasped by the broad masses, it becomes an inexhaustible source of strength and a spiritual atom bomb of infinite power.[7]*

An estimated five billion copies of the pocket-sized book were printed between 1964 and the end of the Cultural Revolution in 1976, making it the most printed book in history.[8] During the Cultural Revolution, studying *Quotations from Chairman Mao Zedong* was required in schools and workplaces. *The Little Red Book* was a ubiquitous part of life in China during the Cultural Revolution. On pages 100–117, Ji-li provides examples of how waving *The Little Red Book* was an integral part of community events, such as Morning Benediction. Reading excerpts from *Quotations from Chairman Mao Zedong* can help students appreciate the ideas that Ji-li and young people throughout China were exposed to during the Cultural Revolution. The entire text of this book has been published by the Internet Archive project (*http://www.archive.org/details/maozedongquotes*). We have selected nine quotations from *The Little Red Book* that are especially appropriate for classroom use. Any of these quotations can be used as prompts for journal writing or classroom discussion. In addition, here are several other ways you might use these quotations to enhance students' understanding of *Red Scarf Girl* and the Cultural Revolution:

> • In small groups or pairs, have students paraphrase Chairman Mao's words. Then they can discuss the degree to which they agree or disagree with the statement.

- Students can select, or be assigned, one quotation to present to the class. Students might be responsible for paraphrasing the quotation, illustrating the quotation (or finding an image that represents the ideas in the quotation), and/or identifying how the ideas in the quotation relate to something they have read in *Red Scarf Girl*.

- After reading and paraphrasing these quotations, students can explore the following questions in writing or in a discussion: What messages do Mao's quotations express about how Chinese, especially Chinese youth, should think and act? Which of these quotations do you most agree with? Which do you most strongly disagree with? Which of these values or beliefs, if any, feel familiar to you?

- **Document 16:** *Point 10 of the "Decision Concerning the Great Proletarian Cultural Revolution" (also known as "The Sixteen Points")*

On August 8, 1966, the leadership of the Chinese Communist Party passed the "Decision Concerning the Great Proletarian Cultural Revolution," which became known as the Sixteen Points. This document outlined Chairman Mao's vision for the Cultural Revolution.[9] Prior to this decision, the Cultural Revolution was, for the most part, a student movement. By calling on "the masses of workers, peasants, soldiers, revolutionary intellectuals, and revolutionary cadres" to "form the main force of the Great Proletarian Cultural Revolution," the Sixteen Points legitimized the Cultural Revolution, broadened its reach, and provided direction about how the revolution should proceed. We have included a brief excerpt of this document: Point 10, which deals exclusively with education. Point 10 emphasizes the need to "reform the old educational system and the old principles and methods of teaching." In *Red Scarf Girl*, especially in chapter 10, Ji-li Jiang describes some of the ways these directions were put into practice. English class consisted of learning how to say phrases such as "Long live Chairman Mao," and "Long live the Chinese Communist Party." Ji-li complained, "It was boring, and we knew that if we did not learn grammar instead of just phrases, we would never learn English" (p. 162). She goes on to describe how the entire curriculum was redesigned to prepare youth for their role as workers and patriotic Communists. Studying Point 10 of the "Decision Concerning the Great Proletarian Cultural Revolution" can help students explore the concept of civic education. After reading this document, students can address questions such as:

- How does this document resonate with what you have read about Ji-li's experience at Xin-zha Junior High School? Find evidence from *Red Scarf Girl* that supports the directions issued in this document.

- What is the role of schools in preparing young people for their role as citizens?

- What does schooling during the Cultural Revolution reveal about Chinese society at that time? What does the education system in your community (local or national) reveal about the culture in which you live?

As a synthesis activity, students can write an educational manifesto, in the style of Point 10, outlining what they think would be appropriate policies by which to direct a national school system. This assignment could be accompanied by oral presentations in which students explain their ideas and take questions from their peers. After these presentations, students could have the opportunity to revise their statements, individually or in groups.

EXTENSIONS

1. **Working with dilemmas:** In *Red Scarf Girl*, members of the Jiang family confront challenging dilemmas. For example, Ji-li's father has to decide whether or not he should confess to crimes he did not commit. Ji-li's mother is asked to lie about her husband in order to save her job. And Ji-li is also asked to betray her family in order to have a bright future. Students can select one of these dilemma moments and write about it in the format of an advice column. First, have students frame the question for the advice columnist in the form of a dilemma. The question should identify at least two important values that are in conflict with each other. Then, have students answer the character's question in the voice of the advice columnist, drawing on evidence from the text, prior knowledge, and their own beliefs and experience. You could also have a group of students collaborate on writing the question but ask each group member to write his or her own answer. Then group members can discuss their answers with each other.

2. **Four-corners debate:** Reading *Red Scarf Girl* and studying the Cultural Revolution raises important questions about the relationship between the individual and society, such as: What does a society's education system reveal about its values and beliefs about citizenship? What should be the relationship between the state and the individual? To whom are individuals most responsible: their state, their family, or themselves? One way to help students develop their own thoughts on these questions is through a *four-corners debate*. (Refer to page 137 for more information about this teaching strategy.) Statements you might use for this activity include:

   • The needs of larger society are more important than the needs of the individual. (Or, in the words of Chang Hong, "[W]e can't allow personal matters to interfere with revolutionary duties.")

   • The purpose of schooling is to prepare youth to be good citizens.

   • Individuals can choose their own destiny; their choices are not dictated or limited by the constraints of society.

   • One should always resist unfair laws, regardless of the consequences.

   • I am only responsible for myself.

[1] "Decision concerning the great proletarian cultural revolution," The Róbinson Rojas Archive website, *http://www.rrojasdatabank.info/16points.htm* (accessed June 4, 2009).

[2] "Campaign for the Civic Mission of Schools," Educating for Democracy website, *http://www.civicmissionofschools.org* (accessed on June 4, 2009).

[3] Feng Jicai, *Voices from the Whirlwind: An Oral History of the Chinese Cultural Revolution* (Pantheon Books, 1991), 100.

[4] David Ashley, *Mao's Children in the New China: Voices From the Red Guard Generation*, ed. Yarong Jiang (Routledge, 2000), 167.

[5] Hao Jiang Tian, *Along the Roaring River: My Wild Ride from Mao to the Met* (John Wiley and Sons Inc., 2008), 62.

[6] Maurice Meisner, *Mao's China and After: A History of the People's Republic*, 3rd ed. (The Free Press, 1999), 280.

[7] Lin Piao, "Forward to the Second Edition," *Quotations from Chairman Mao Tse-Tung* (Foreign Language Press, 1967).

[8] Zhengyuan Fu, *Autocratic Tradition and Chinese Politics* (Cambridge University Press, 1993), 186.

[9] Roderick MacFarquar, *The Politics of China: The Eras of Mau and Deng*, 2nd ed. (Cambridge University Press, 1997), 178.

DOCUMENT 15

Selected "Quotations from Chairman Mao Zedong": *The Little Red Book* [1]

1. *We are not only good at destroying the old world, we are also good at building the new.*

2. *Everyone lives as a member of a particular class, and every kind of thinking, without exception, is stamped with the brand of a class.*

3. *There are not a few people who are irresponsible in their work, preferring the light to the heavy, shoving the heavy loads on to others and choosing the easy ones for themselves. At every turn they think of themselves before others. . . . In truth such people are not Communists, or at least cannot be counted as true Communists.*

4. *It is up to us to organize the people. As for the **reactionaries** in China, it is up to us to organize the people to overthrow them. Everything reactionary is the same; if you don't hit it, it won't fall. It is like sweeping the floor; where the broom does not reach, the dust never vanishes of itself.*

5. *A revolution is not a dinner party, or writing an essay, or painting a picture, or doing embroidery; it cannot be so **refined**, so leisurely and gentle, so **temperate**, kind, courteous, restrained and **magnanimous**. A revolution is an **insurrection**, an act of violence by which one class overthrows another.*

6. *Because of their lack of political and social experience, quite a number of young people are unable to see the contrast between the old China and the new, and it is not easy for them thoroughly to comprehend the hardships our people went through in the struggle to free themselves from the oppression of the **imperialists and Kuomintang reactionaries**, or the long period of **arduous** work needed before a happy **socialist** society can be established. That is why we must constantly carry on lively and effective political education among the masses, and should always tell them the truth about the difficulties that crop up, and discuss with them how to **surmount** these difficulties.*

7. *How should we judge whether a youth is a revolutionary? How can we tell? There can only be one criterion, namely, whether or not he is willing to integrate himself with the broad masses of workers and peasants, and does so in practice.*

8. *Protect the interests of the youth, women, and children—provide assistance to young students who cannot afford to continue their studies, help the youth and women to organize in order to participate on equal footing in all work useful to the war effort and to social progress, ensure freedom of marriage and equality as between men and women, and give young people and children a useful education . . .*

9. *The world is yours, as well as ours, but in the last analysis, it is yours. You young people, full of **vigor and vitality**, are in the bloom of life, like the sun at eight or nine in the morning. Our hope is placed on you.*

GLOSSARY

arduous: difficult

imperialists and Koumintang reactionaries: those who want to return to the time before 1949, when foreign powers and a small Chinese elite controlled China

insurrection: a violent uprising against the established way of life

magnanimous: overly kind and forgiving

reactionaries: those who are against the Communist revolution

refined: orderly

socialist: pertaining to a society where the good of the whole group is seen as more important than the needs of the individual

surmount: overcome

temperate: calm and even-keeled, not showing strong emotions

vigor and vitality: strength and energy

DOCUMENT 16

Point 10 of the "Decision Concerning the Great Proletarian Cultural Revolution" (also known as the "Sixteen Points"): "Education" [2]

In the Great Proletarian Cultural Revolution a most important task is to transform the old educational system, and the old principles and methods of teaching.

In this Great Cultural Revolution, the **phenomenon** of our schools being dominated by **bourgeois intellectuals** must be completely changed.

In every kind of school we must apply thoroughly the policy advanced by Comrade Mao Tse-tung of education serving proletarian politics, and education being combined with productive labor, so as to enable those receiving an education to develop morally, intellectually, and physically and to become laborers with **socialist consciousness** and culture.

The period of schooling should be shortened. Courses should be fewer and better. The teaching material should be thoroughly transformed, in some cases beginning with simplifying complicated material. While their main task is to study, students should also learn other things. That is to say, in addition to their studies they should also learn industrial work, farming, and military affairs, and take part in the struggles of the Cultural Revolution to criticize the bourgeoisie as these struggles occur.

GLOSSARY

phenomenon: situation

bourgeois intellectuals: middle-class people, often shopkeepers, landlords, and professionals (teachers, doctors, etc.) who work with their brains more than their hands; the Communist Party viewed them as not understanding or supporting the perspective of factory workers, laborers, farmers, and peasants

socialist consciousness: an ability to understand the benefits of the socialist system, a system that gives priority to the good of the whole group over the needs of the individual

---

[1] Mao Tse-Tung, *Quotations from Chairman Mao Tse-Tung: The Little Red Book* (Foreign Language Press, 1970).

[2] "Decision concerning the great proletarian cultural revolution," The Róbinson Rojas Archive website, *http://www.rrojasdatabank.info/16points.htm* (accessed June 9, 2009).

PART 5: CHOICES AND THEIR CONSEQUENCES

Includes chapters "Half-City Jiangs" (pp. 206–217), "The Class Education Exhibition" (pp. 218–229), "The Rice Harvest" (pp. 230–243), "The Incriminating Letter" (pp. 244–259), and "Sweeping" (pp. 260–264)

OVERVIEW

In the final chapters of *Red Scarf Girl*, Ji-li confronts a series of difficult ethical decisions that require her to consider the range of options available and the consequences of her actions for herself, her family, and her society. For example, now that the Jiangs have been publicly accused of being landlords, should Ji-li "make a clean break" with her "black family" by changing her family name? What should she do when she is asked to prove her "revolutionary determination" by testifying against her own father? Should Ji-li volunteer to work in the countryside to "wash the black stain" from her back, even though her family needs her help in the city? Finally, how should Ji-li respond when her mother asks her to hide a letter critical of the Cultural Revolution? What should she do when officials threaten to beat her elderly grandmother if she does not reveal the location of this "incriminating letter"?

The types of choices Ji-li confronts were not unusual for children who grew up during the Cultural Revolution. In his memoir *Born Red*, Gao Yuan, the son of a Communist official, shares how he questioned his father's loyalty to the revolution and considered breaking ties with him. In a letter, his father responded, "I have devoted my life to the cause of the revolution . . . I am hopeful that you will have faith in me. However, if for the time being you believe that I am a capitalist-roader, as some people charge, you may abandon me. I will not complain."[1] Gao Yuan ultimately decided to remain in his family. Other young people, like Ji-li's cousin Shan-shan, decide to break with their families. Surely, the choices of Chinese youth were influenced by the songs, posters, films, and other forms of propaganda expressing the idea that "father and mother are dear, but dearer still is Chairman Mao." Throughout *Red Scarf Girl*, Ji-li is bombarded with messages from teachers, peers, and other officials about how she is the child of Mao. This message represents a fundamental shift in Chinese culture. Prior to the Cultural Revolution, loyalty to family came before self. During the Cultural Revolution, however, allegiance to Mao took priority over loyalty to family or self.

Ji-li is not the only character in *Red Scarf Girl* whose behaviors merit attention. Students can also reflect on how others' actions impact Ji-li and her family. Some people's choices harm the Jiang family: Uncle Zhu falsely testifies against Ji-li's father, and Thin-Face leads the raid on the Jiang home. Why might they have made these decisions? Self-preservation, obedience to authority, fear, conformity, and the influence of propaganda are all factors that may have influenced these choices. Recalling his experience growing up during the Cultural Revolution, Hao Jian Tian writes, "Human relationships being what they are, people also found a potent tool to get revenge on their enemies, those with whom they were competing for higher rank and privilege—or others whom they wanted to bring down."[2]

At the same time, Ji-li also describes the large and small ways that people in her community try to help her and her family: Song Po-po continues to mop their floors; Chang Hong tries to "rescue" Ji-li's reputation; and Bai Shan offers to help Ji-li harvest rice. Why might they have made these choices to help the Jiang family, even when they could have suffered for helping "landlords"? What helped these characters see the Jiangs as distinct individuals, not as "evil landlords"? Why were they able to see their humanity and treat them accordingly when others did not? Might their behavior be considered acts of resistance to Mao and the Cultural Revolution?

Red Scarf Girl is a story about the Cultural Revolution. It is also, however, a story about the moral development of a young girl as she grows into adulthood. Ji-li started this story as a "lucky" 12-year-old girl with a "perfect" life. She ended this story as a 14-year-old teenager living in an empty apartment, her father in jail and her grandmother forced to sweep the alley. Through the many choices Ji-li is forced to make along this journey, she learns important lessons about fairness, prejudice, and belonging. Most importantly, she learns about responsibility. At the end of her memoir, Ji-li writes, "Once my life had been defined by my goals . . . Now my life was defined by my responsibilities" (p. 263). With this statement, she recognizes how her universe of responsibility has expanded to include not just herself and her dedication to Chairman Mao but also her family. Through writing this memoir, Ji-li Jiang expands her universe of responsibility further to include all of us—her readers—with whom she wants to share this story. In a letter to students, Ji-li Jiang explains:

> *I hope that by sharing my story with you, not only will you remember the darkest time in modern Chinese history, but also that you will realize that this kind of tragedy is universal, and similar tragedies are actually still happening every day. The importance of learning history is not the history itself, but how we apply history's lessons to our own lives to prevent further tragedies from occurring.[3]*

Hopefully, like Ji-li, your students will emerge from adolescence with a broader sense of their role in society. Evaluating the choices made by Ji-li and other characters in *Red Scarf Girl* can help students reflect on their own universe of responsibility and the impact their choices have on others—their peers, families, and the larger community.

ESSENTIAL QUESTIONS

> *Civic participation is often defined as individual or group actions to influence issues of public concern. How can civic participation contribute to positive outcomes? Under what conditions can civic participation contribute to negative outcomes? What kind of civic participation should be encouraged? What kind of civic participation should be discouraged?*

> *How do individuals, groups, and nations decide whom to include in their "universe of responsibility"—the people whom they feel an obligation to care and protect? What are the consequences for individuals and groups who are considered outside of a community's universe of responsibility?*

> *What are ways that groups and individuals resist authority? Under what conditions is it appropriate to resist authority?*

What does it mean to be an upstander? What encourages and inspires people to stand up to injustice? What prevents or discourages upstander behavior?

SUGGESTED ACTIVITIES

DISCUSSIONS AND JOURNAL WRITING

For chapter 13, "Half–City Jiangs" (pp. 206–217)

When Ji-li hears about the article about the Jiang family in the *Workers' Revolt* newspaper, one of her first thoughts is "Everybody read the *Workers' Revolt*," and then she spills her tea before storming out of her house (page 211). Based on Ji-li's reaction, what power do you think the media, such as newspapers, had in terms of influencing public opinion in China during the Cultural Revolution? To what extent does the media control or influence public opinion in society today?

After the article about the Jiang family is published, Ji-li runs out of her house. On her walk, she passes the police station and decides to enter to change her name, telling herself, "No! I did not want to have this damned name any more! I had had enough. All my bad luck and humiliation came from the name Jiang" (p. 212). What does the name Jiang represent to Ji-li? What does this name represent to others in the story? What is the symbolism of Ji-li wanting to change her name? What is the significance of the fact that she ultimately decides not to change her name? What does your name represent to you? Under what conditions would you consider changing your name?

Compare the behavior of Song Po-po at the end of this chapter to the behavior of Pudge on page 212. What might explain why Song Po-po helps the Jiang family, despite their background, while Ji-li's classmates tease her and call her names? Under what conditions are you most likely to help others?

For chapter 14, "The Class Education Exhibition" (pp. 218–229)

In chapter 10, when Ji-li is asked to become a member of the propaganda group for the school newspaper, she decides not to join. Yet, even after the article in the *Workers' Revolt* publicly criticizes the Jiang family, Ji-li does not shy away from her role in the Class Education Exhibition. Rather, she explains, "I had been seized by a new determination not to give in to pressure . . . I had to win my honor back" (pp. 218–219). How can you explain Ji-li's change in attitude? What do you think she means when she says she wants to win her honor back? What is honor? How is it lost? How do you gain it back? From whom?

On page 221, Chairman Jin says, "This Class Education Exhibition is a very powerful weapon." How was education being used in China during the Cultural Revolution? Do you think education was a "powerful weapon" in this context? What about in your own society today?

When the foreman from Ji-li's father's workplace is at school to question Ji-li, he tells her, "Now, you have to choose between two roads. You can break with your family and follow Chairman Mao, or you can follow your father and become an enemy of the people" (p. 226). To what extent do you agree with the foreman that Ji-li must choose between only "two roads"? Can you think of any other options (or "roads") available to Ji-li? At this moment, Ji-li faces an incredible dilemma. Have you ever confronted a difficult decision or a dilemma? What did it feel like? What helped you make a decision?

For chapter 15, "The Rice Harvest" (pp. 230–243)

Ji-li decides to join her classmates in the countryside, even though she knows she is needed at home in the city to help take care of her family. Previously, Ji-li had made decisions that protected her family above all else. How can you explain her decision to work in the countryside? How is this decision different from some of the others she has confronted?

When Ji-li is struggling to finish her work in the fields, she rejects Bai Shan's offers of help. Why do you think she does this? Have you ever rejected help from someone? Why? Under what conditions do you think it is appropriate to accept help from others?

What is the meaning of Ji-li's dream (p. 241)? Why do you think she wanted to include this dream in her memoir? What does it add to the story?

For chapter 16, "The Incriminating Letter" (pp. 244–259)

In chapter 16, Ji-li's mother, in collaboration with others, writes a letter to the Municipal Party Committee to complain about unfair conditions in her workplace. Why would she write the letter? What risks is she taking? What does she have to gain? What does Ji-li's mother's decision reveal about how she defines her universe of responsibility?

The Jiang family suffers serious consequences because of the "incriminating letter." Their house is ransacked, Grandma is physically attacked, all of their furniture is taken, and they are reclassified. Do you think any of these characters regret their actions? What is a reasonable price to pay for your ideals?

On page 258, we learn that Ji-li's mother "had now been classified as a landlord's wife." In the context of the Cultural Revolution, what does it mean to be reclassified? What are the implications of living in a society where the government can decide who belongs and who does not belong? Under what conditions, if any, do you think it is appropriate for the government to classify people? For example, should governments be able to decide who is and is not a citizen? If so, how should governments make this decision?

For chapter 17, "Sweeping" (pp. 260–264)

On page 263, Ji-li writes, "Once my life had been defined by my goals . . . Now my life was defined by my responsibilities." What do you think has happened over the past two years to inspire this change in Ji-li? What does it mean for someone's life to be defined by their responsibilities? What is your life defined by?

What was Ji-li's relationship to the Cultural Revolution? Would you describe Ji-li's character as a perpetrator, victim, bystander, and/or upstander?

Ji-li ends the main story with the words "I will do my job. I will." What do you think she is referring to when she says this? Why do you think she chose to end the book this way? What do you think happened next in her life?

Based on what you know about the Cultural Revolution from 1966 to 1968 (the years covered in *Red Scarf Girl*), do you think this movement was a success? What did the leaders of the Cultural Revolution and their followers want to achieve? To what extent do you think they achieved their goals?

USING DOCUMENTS: EXPLORING "UP TO THE MOUNTAINS, DOWN TO THE VILLAGES"

In chapter 15, Ji-li describes being sent to the countryside to work in the fields. Her experience represents that of millions of urban youth living in China during the Cultural Revolution. In December 1968, Mao called for the urban youth to go "Up to the Mountains and Down to the Villages," where they would be reeducated through hard work alongside peasants in the countryside. After two years of disrupted classes in the middle schools and universities and clashes among the Red Guards, Mao's campaign served to subdue the large numbers of urban youth who had been radicalized by the Cultural Revolution. Relocation and reeducation of urban youth was not a new practice; 1.2 million youth were sent to rural villages between 1956 and 1966 to contribute to the growth of the country and participate in the ongoing revolution. However, the campaign increased in intensity during the Cultural Revolution. Between 1968 and 1975, over 12 million young people—roughly 10 percent of the urban youth population in 1970— were relocated from urban areas to the countryside. Propaganda images at the time represented wholesome youth in an idyllic rural setting and conveyed the message that urban youth would thrive while living amidst peasants and devoting themselves to the Communist Party.

In reality, many in the "sent-down" generation were unprepared for rural life and suffered from the harsh conditions of manual labor and from hunger. Once the Cultural Revolution ended, many sent-down youth stayed in the countryside where they had made a life, but most eventually made their way back to the city, particularly as the economy became more open in the 1980s. Because they had missed years of education, they became known as the "lost generation." Many members of this generation had difficulty finding decent employment, and only about five percent were able to attend college. Despite lacking years of education, quite a few members of the sent-down generation have become successful entrepreneurs, and some have become politically involved both as members of the Chinese leadership and as democracy activists who challenge the government and are frequently arrested.[4]

• **Document 17:** *Firsthand accounts from the "sent-down" generation*

We have selected three excerpts from interviews with Chinese adults who were sent to the countryside when they were teenagers. These firsthand accounts portray different perspectives on the experience of being "sent down."

• **Document 18:** *"Learn from Dazhai, work hard to make great changes," poster (1975)*

Posters like this one were also widely disseminated by the government to promote the "Up to the Mountains, Down to the Villages" campaign. This poster focuses on Dazhai, a small farming town that was selected to become a model of new collective farming methods. Mao's "Learn from Dazhai in agriculture" campaign was intended to promote the work ethic and farming methods implemented in Dazhai. Farmers from across China were organized to tour Dazhai, and books, newspaper articles, songs, and films were distributed nationally.

Students can learn about the "Up to the Mountains, Down to the Villages" campaign by studying two types of sources: firsthand accounts of "sent-down" youth and a government-issued poster. After interpreting what these sources reveal about this campaign, students can discuss the following questions:

- Who created these documents? What were their motivations? How might their motives influence their portrayal of the "Up to the Mountains, Down to the Villages" campaign?

- Which of these documents do you think is most true or valid? Why?

- When historians confront sources that provide different perspectives of the same event, how should they take this into account?

- As a final activity, students could create their own description of the "Up to the Mountains, Down to the Villages" campaign, based on these documents and *Red Scarf Girl.* How do they choose to explain what happened? Which perspectives will they emphasize? Why did they make this choice? Answering these questions puts students in the position of doing the work of historians.

EXTENSIONS

1. **Using *identity charts* to understand change and continuity:** In *Red Scarf Girl*, Ji-li Jiang describes her life at the beginning of the Cultural Revolution, between 1966 and 1968. Reflecting on these two years in her life, Ji-li writes in the last chapter, "Once my life had been defined by my goals . . . Now my life was defined by my responsibilities." After students finish reading chapter 17, ask them to draw an identity chart for Ji-li. They can compare this chart to the identity chart they created for her at the beginning of the memoir. What is the same? What has changed? This exercise provides a springboard to a conversation about why and how Ji-li's character has changed in the past two years. Thinking about how Ji-li's identity was influenced by growing up during the Cultural Revolution provides an opportunity for students to consider the events, and other factors, that may have shaped their own identities. Students can imagine that they created an identity chart for themselves two years ago and were comparing it to an identity chart they made for themselves today. How has their identity changed over the past two years? What has influenced these changes? These are questions students can answer in a journal entry or in a conversation with a small group of peers.

2. **Design an exhibition:** In chapter 14, we read about the Class Education Exhibition that Ji-li and her classmates create for the purpose of teaching students and community members about Mao Zedong's thought. Ji-li's exhibit used a powerful story about an evil landlord to send the message that class struggle is necessary to end the oppression of peasants. If students were asked to design an exhibition to teach about values important to society today, what message would they want the exhibit to express? What stories might they want to include? Students can develop plans for these exhibits in small groups and then share them with the rest of the class.

3. **Illustrate a scene:** Ji-li Jiang uses dialogue, figurative language, actions, and thoughts to help create vivid scenes. Yet, the words on a page often translate differently as images in our minds. One way to test this theory is to ask students to illustrate particular moments in the story. Specific scenes students might consider illustrating include the following:

- Ji-li talks to Officer Ma at the police station (pp. 213–215)

- Ji-li harvests the first crop of rice (pp. 234–237)

- Thin-Face confronts Ji-li during the raid (pp. 251–254)

Planning these drawings requires students to look closely at the text and can therefore help students become more aware of how authors use language to create scenes in the readers' minds. This exercise also helps students appreciate how readers interpret the same words in different ways. As an extension of this activity, students can compose their own scenes and then trade their scenes with partners, who illustrate them. After the illustrations are complete, pairs can discuss the extent to which the drawing corresponds to the image in the author's mind when writing the scene. Not only does this exercise help students develop a sense of what clear, detailed writing is, but it also raises questions about literary interpretation, such as "Is it possible for the reader and the author to draw different meanings from the same text? Can both interpretations be 'right'?"

[1] Yuan Gao, *Born Red: A Chronicle of the Cultural Revolution* (Stanford University Press, 1987), 143.

[2] Hao Jiang Tian, *Along the Roaring River: My Wild Ride from Mao to the Met* (John Wiley and Sons Inc., 2008), 31.

[3] "Letter from Ji-li Jiang," *China's Cultural Revolution*, Gregory Francis and Stefanie Lamb, Developers (SPICE Stanford, 2005), 160.

[4] Leah Caprice, "The Lost Generation of the 17th Chinese Communist Party Politburo," *China Brief*, Volume 8, Issue 19 (October 7, 2008);
http://www.jamestown.org/programs/chinabrief/single/?tx_ttnews[tt_news]=5210&tx_ttnews[backPid]=168&no_cache=1.

DOCUMENT 17

Firsthand accounts of "sent-down" generation

Interview #1 (Lu Xin)

In 1968, I went to Heilongjiang province. I could have waited another year, but I was determined to go to the countryside, and wanted to leave as soon as possible. My eldest brother was one of those idealistic students who left to serve peasants in Xinjiang province before the Cultural Revolution began. When he got tuberculosis, he had to return to Shanghai for treatment. After he recovered, he persuaded several unemployed young people from our neighborhood to return to Xinjiang with him. He was a great influence on me. I thought I was going to change the backwardness of our countryside and transform the whole world. I was, of course, very innocent . . .

*When millions of educated young people moved to the countryside, they did begin to stimulate some changes, no matter how small these were. The students were the losers because they sacrificed their education. The countryside offered no hope of personal advancement. But we willingly adjusted to the harsh conditions. All our energy was consumed by the **primitive**, endless labor. In winter, the temperature could fall to minus 40° centigrade. I didn't have a pair of boots or a sheepskin coat. My cotton-filled coat was useless because, after a couple of years, the cotton hardened into big lumps. The cold was unbearable, but we still had to work outside or in an unheated room. I was not spoiled as a child, but, before I joined the peasants, I'd never experienced real hardship.*[1]

Interview #2 (Wan Jinli)

*Like most other students, I participated in all kinds of activities at the beginning of the Cultural Revolution. I didn't want to be left out. However, I felt lost. There was no authority anymore. Previously, the teachers and the school authorities had always praised me. In return, I respected them and took pride in myself. Now, my teachers could no longer give me the sense of purpose and identity I needed. I think this is why I was so excited by the "Up to the Mountains and Down to the Villages" movement . . . At one meeting I attended, I heard a speech by an official from **Anhui**. He told us how much we were needed in those poor regions. In my mind, I saw myself as a new type of peasant, transforming the countryside . . .*

Nearly 4,000 students were sent to Nanqin County in Anhui province . . . My production team was the Little Autumn Village, which had more than 100 residents. Before we arrived the only person who could read was the production team's Accounts Recorder. He'd had about three years of schooling. We had to adjust to a completely different environment. . . . The best building in the village was the storage barn, parts of which were constructed with brick. The peasants' houses were made of mud and straw . . . It was bare poverty. Everyone was shocked by what we found. . .

*Obviously, we weren't going to get much material help from the peasants. We had to figure out for ourselves how best to survive . . . We lived on corn for two weeks . . . We knew nothing about **horticulture**, but the first thing we did was to study those books on agricultural technology. The peasants in the village had been planting the same crops and vegetables for generations . . . During our first year we grew eggplants, beans, melons, tomatoes, and Shanghai-style cabbage. We read the books, put the knowledge into practice and saw the fruit of our labors . . . We could read, you see— that made . . . a difference . . . I've always believed that the "Up to the Mountains and Down to the Villages" movement served to bring the fresh culture of educated youth into the countryside. This was a very good thing. For the first time ever, local people who had never even seen a city had some contact with urban culture.[2]*

Interview #3 (the deputy commander of a state farm)

*In 1969, when the call came to go to the countryside, I was the first to sign up . . . I remember the scene perfectly: The station was filled with people seeing everybody off with drums and gongs. Of course, some people did shed tears. But there was no sense of **banishment**, just the natural feelings when family members parted. The students on the train all helped each other out—everybody was chummy. . . . We sang or recited quotes from Mao and shouted slogans all the way. The train was really alive with singing and dancing. For the great majority of us, it was the first time we'd ridden on a train in our lives. It was refreshing to watch the beauty of the landscape of our motherland along the way. It made us feel even more strongly that this was the only road for educated youth to take. That's the way we thought.*

*When we got to the Great Northern Wilderness, the first problem we faced was that working conditions were too harsh. The first real, direct challenge was survival itself. . . . Working with empty stomachs, we got tired easily. The more tired we got, the hungrier we'd be, and the hungrier we were, the harder it was to get full—it was a **vicious cycle**. We had to get up every morning at three or four, and we worked till dark.*

*The farm had paddy fields and its level of **mechanization** was extremely low. All the tilling, sowing, and reaping had to be done manually. People were the machines. In the northwest, you prepare for planting in May, and first you have to till the land. For that you had to wear shorts, and on top you wore a cotton-padded jacket. Although the ice on top was completely melted and the water was only just over ten centimeters deep, the ground beneath was all mud and ice, and your feet got all cut up. I don't know if it was the ice or the cold water, but with the wind on top of that, your legs froze and the skin was covered with little cuts. One year I went home after spring planting. When my mother saw that the whole lower half of my body was covered with cuts, she felt so bad she cried.[3]*

GLOSSARY

Anhui: a region of China

banishment: being forced to leave a place

horticulture: the science of growing plants, particularly fruits and vegetables

mechanization: the use of machines

primitive: simple and crude

vicious cycle: a terrible situation that does not end because one trouble leads to another

---

[1] David Ashley, *Mao's Children in the New China: Voices From the Red Guard Generation*, ed. Yarong Jiang (Routledge, 2000), 14.

[2] Ibid., 54–56.

[3] Feng Jicai, *Voices from the Whirlwind: An Oral History of the Chinese Cultural Revolution* (Pantheon Books, 1991), 6–9.

101

PART 6: LEGACY

Includes the Epilogue (pp. 265–272)

OVERVIEW

Reading *Red Scarf Girl* demonstrates that by studying someone else's history—by "walking in their shoes"—we can learn about ourselves and our society. Reading *Red Scarf Girl* also reveals the power of using personal stories to shed light on important historical moments and universal aspects of human behavior. From this memoir of one young girl in China, we are able to learn about how a nation can be turned upside down when power goes unchecked by a "sound legal system" or a critical citizenry. At the same time, we also learn about the desire to belong, the shame of exclusion, the power of propaganda, the inclination to follow authority, and the courage to resist. By giving us access to her story, Ji-li Jiang invites us to better understand our own stories, and our society today.

Jiang's particular history during the Cultural Revolution, influenced by her family, her friendships, her aspirations, her talents, and her unique set of experiences, impacts her memory and her judgment of the past. In the epilogue, she remembers those years as ones of brainwashing, denied opportunities, and government abuse. Reading *Red Scarf Girl*, a memoir told from the viewpoint of a relatively privileged Chinese woman who has lived in the United States since 1984, demands that we remind ourselves of the role perspective plays in how history gets written, taught, and remembered. Others who grew up during the Cultural Revolution recall this time as "the happiest period of my life."[1] Former Red Guards now form the backbone of a group of independent thinkers, and some argue that the recent economic and social development would not have been possible without the Cultural Revolution. Thus, it is impossible to describe a singular legacy of the Cultural Revolution; this decade is remembered differently based on the distinct experiences of millions of Chinese, all of whom have stories that can be appreciated, discussed, accepted, and disputed.

In 1981, the Chinese Communist Party declared its official stance on the legacy of the Cultural Revolution by publicly acknowledging that this movement was wrong and caused great damage to China. Chairman Mao was retroactively blamed for making political and ideological mistakes that made the Cultural Revolution possible. The worst crimes of the time were blamed on a group called the "Gang of Four"* that consisted of Mao's wife, Jiang Qing, and three other radical leaders of the CCP.[2] With this announcement, many Chinese who had been jailed as reactionaries and rightists were rehabilitated. Those who died were "posthumously rehabilitated" with apologies offered to their families. Were these actions sufficient? Who should be held accountable for the terrible suffering and destruction committed during the Cultural Revolution? How can society heal after such enormous social and political conflict? In the epilogue of *Red Scarf Girl*, Ji-li Jiang responds to some of these questions. There are those, like Jiang,

---

*Jian Qing: wife of Mao Zedong and Politburo member (1973–1976); Wang Hongwen: former textile mill worker who became Vice-Chairman of the CCP in 1973; Yao Wenyuan, editor at the Shanghai Liberation Daily, who became a Politburo member in 1973; Zhang Qunqiao, secretary of CCP Shanghai Municipal Committee, who became a Politburo member in 1973 and then Vice Premier of the State Council in 1975.

who are frustrated that only the leaders of the Cultural Revolution, the "Gang of Four," were held responsible for the atrocities committed during the Cultural Revolution. One victim of the Cultural Revolution shared, "Don't tell me that it was all the fault of the Gang of Four. If it was just the Gang of Four without the crowds, they could not have caused such massive evil."[3] On the other hand, many Chinese do not believe former Red Guards were at fault. They argue that young Chinese were brainwashed since birth to follow Mao, and that they were only following orders. The roles of victims and perpetrators switched often enough during the Cultural Revolution to cause "moral and historical confusion," according to Professor Wang Youqin.[4] Drawing from the ideas of Ji-li Jiang and others (see document 19), students can begin to form their own ideas about the legacy of the Cultural Revolution. This exploration can help students develop their own views about justice and forgiveness in society, and in their own lives.

ESSENTIAL QUESTIONS

What is justice after a national conflict? Who should be held responsible for events that affect an entire society? Are individuals responsible for their crimes if they were following the orders of their leaders?

What helps societies heal after years of conflict and violence?

What can be learned from studying other people's histories? What does it mean to "learn from the past?" After learning about moments of violence and injustice from the past, what can we do to make sure history does not repeat itself?

SUGGESTED ACTIVITIES

DISCUSSIONS AND JOURNAL WRITING

For the epilogue, (pp. 265–272)

"We were all brainwashed," Ji-li declares on page 265. What does it mean to be brainwashed? What evidence does she provide in *Red Scarf Girl* to support the view that her generation was brainwashed? What can people, including young people, do to avoid being brainwashed?

On page 266, Ji-li argues, "Without a sound legal system, a small group or even a single person can take control of an entire country." What do you think she means by a "sound legal system"? What made the legal system unsound in China during the 1960s? How do you think a sound legal system can be used to prevent dictatorship and oligarchy (control of a government by one group)? Do you think your society has a sound legal system? Why or why not?

Ji-li explains that many of those who physically and/or emotionally tortured others during the Cultural Revolution were never formally judged and punished. She writes, "Those who persecuted others, even beat or tortured them, were victims too, after all"

(p. 270). What do you think she means by this statement? To what extent do you agree or disagree with the idea that the perpetrators of violence were also the victims? Do you think it is fair or appropriate that former Red Guards have not been formally judged and held accountable for their actions? Why or why not?

Ji-li writes that she hopes this book will serve her mission to contribute something to China and America. What might this "something" be? What do you think Ji-li has achieved by writing this memoir? Who benefits from its publication?

Why is it important for individuals to share their history through writing a book (or making a film, publishing a website, creating music, etc.)? What are the consequences if people keep silent about the past?

Ji-li Jiang wrote this book in English for an American audience. How can this story be of value to youth who are growing up in a different time and place? How might this book be received differently in the United States and in China? In China, memoirs like *Red Scarf Girl* are classified as "scar literature." What does this phrase mean to you? Why do you think some Chinese would label *Red Scarf Girl* this way?

What did you learn about yourself and society today from reading *Red Scarf Girl*? What messages do you take away from Ji-li Jiang's story?

USING DOCUMENTS: THE LEGACY OF THE CULTURAL REVOLUTION[5]

1976 marked the official end of the Cultural Revolution. A month after Chairman Mao's death in September, Premier Hua Guofeng, the person whom Mao had chosen to succeed him as head of the Chinese Communist Party (CCP) with the support of key political and military figures, arrested the Gang of Four, the leaders of the Cultural Revolution. In a widely publicized trial that resulted in long-term prison sentences, the Gang of Four was held accountable for the atrocities committed during this decade-long campaign. Determining guilt and responsibility for crimes committed during the Cultural Revolution was and is complicated. The same Red Guards who perpetrated violent acts were also victims of the Cultural Revolution. Thousands of individuals who raided homes, stole property, and were responsible for acts of physical or psychological torture remain unpunished. When Deng Xiaoping, purged during the Cultural Revolution from his position as one of the highest ranking leaders of the CCP, returned to power in 1977, his social and economic reforms turned the country in a new direction. In 1981, the CCP adopted a resolution that retroactively placed the blame for the wrongdoings of the Cultural Revolution on Mao Zedong and rehabilitated many of his political opponents who had been jailed or disgraced during the Cultural Revolution.

While the Cultural Revolution came to a close in 1976, its legacy endures. It is difficult to say how many Chinese suffered as a result of the Cultural Revolution. According to the China Rights Forum, millions of Chinese were subjected to persecution and violence, and at least one million Chinese lost their lives as punishment for counterrevolutionary activities. Many committed suicide. Moreover, millions of Chinese adolescents were denied a full education when schools closed and they were sent to the countryside to work. Accounts from former Red Guards often reveal resentment and pain when they reflect on the coercive political tactics used to influence their thinking and behavior at the time.

One legacy of the Cultural Revolution is a robust commitment to education. An entire Chinese generation was denied the right to an education, a right articulated in the Universal Declaration of Human Rights. When schools reopened in 1977, millions of young Chinese took university entrance exams. Of the 5.7 million who took the 1977 exam, only 300,000 were admitted to universities. Many of these students have become part of China's cultural, political, and business elite, and others have become political dissidents and democracy activists. Their experiences during the Cultural Revolution have shaped their ideals, often in terms of embracing more intellectual and economic freedom than they experienced in their youth. Some argue that the policies advanced by this generation have resulted in the economic progress China has enjoyed over the past three decades.

Many questions remain about what happened during the Cultural Revolution and its influence on China today. Little mention is made in Chinese textbooks or classrooms of the atrocities committed between 1967 and 1976. While Western and expatriate Chinese scholars examine this period in history from abroad, scholars within mainland China have met with harassment and imprisonment for studying the Cultural Revolution. In 2006, on the fortieth anniversary of the onset of the Cultural Revolution, the Chinese Communist Party asked scholars and journalists to "ignore the topic."[6] However, the emergence of the Internet has made it possible for more scholars within China to publish research and data about this tumultuous decade.[7] As more information about this period comes to light, the legacy of the Cultural Revolution continues to evolve.

- **Document 19:** The legacy of the Cultural Revolution, selected quotations

This collection of 11 quotations represents a range of perspectives on the Cultural Revolution, from the official statement of the Communist Party to activists to the voices of ordinary Chinese citizens. These quotations can be used to help students understand the legacy of the Cultural Revolution. You might begin by having students read the quotations aloud, one after another, without stopping to call on the next student or to comment. Following the reading of quotations, students can write a journal entry responding to questions such as: What strikes you about these quotations? What ideas do they have in common? What different perspectives on the Cultural Revolution did you hear? You might also ask students to respond to a particular quotation that interests them by answering questions such as: What do you find interesting about this quotation? What does it make you think about? To what extent can you relate to the ideas expressed in this statement? These journal entries serve as preparation for a class discussion about issues of justice and memory following the Cultural Revolution. An exploration of justice and reconciliation in this historical context can help students clarify their own views about justice in society and in their own lives.

EXTENSIONS

Reflections: While reading *Red Scarf Girl* offers a window into a particular moment in history, it also provides an opportunity for students to reflect on issues such as membership, conformity, obedience, responsibility, loyalty, and civic participation in their own lives. Students can create a *da-zi-bao* proclaiming a personally relevant message that they take away from their study of the Cultural Revolution.

Memoir reading and writing: After the completion of *Red Scarf Girl*, it is an appropriate time for students to reflect on the genre of memoir. You might ask them to consider the similarities and differences among several forms of personal nonfiction writing, including biography, diaries, and memoir. Students can compare *Red Scarf Girl* to other memoirs they have read. They can also discuss the role of trust between the reader of a memoir and the author. What did Ji-li Jiang do in *Red Scarf Girl* to make her story believable? Once the class has defined this genre, you can give them the opportunity to be memoirists. Ask students to select an experience or moment from their life that they would like to share with others. Be sure to establish clear guidelines about the topics that are appropriate for their memoirs, especially if students will be expected to share their work publicly.

China after the Cultural Revolution: The documentary *Young and Restless in China* by filmmaker Sue Williams portrays the life of nine young women and men in China today. Watching this film provides an excellent springboard for a discussion about how much life in China has changed since 1968, when Ji-li Jiang ends *Red Scarf Girl*. Students could hypothesize what Ji-li's life might have been like had she been born after the Cultural Revolution. Members of the Facing History network can borrow *Young and Restless in China* from our lending library. The Chinese film *Examination 1977* looks at the legacy of the Cultural Revolution through its focus on the lifting of the decade-long ban on university entrance exams. According to one review, this film "shows not only an individual's desperate pursuit of changes in life, but also represents a nation's respect and craving for knowledge after a decade-long tumultuous period."[8]

---

[1] David Ashley, *Mao's Children in the New China: Voices from the Red Guard Generation,* ed. Yarong Jiang (Routledge, 2000), 13. For other positive accounts of the Cultural Revolution, see the following: Dongping Han, *The Unknown Cultural Revolution: Life and Change in a Chinese Village* (Monthly Review Press, 2008); Mobo Gao, *The Battle for China's Past: Mao and the Cultural Revolution* (Pluto Press, 2008); Xueping Zhong, Wang Zheng, and Bai Di, eds., *Some of Us: Chinese Women Growing Up in the Mao Era* (Rutgers University Press, 2001).

[2] Jiang Qing was deputy director of the Cultural Revolution Group, which was the most powerful leadership organization in China from 1966 to 1969, and a member of the CCP Politburo (1973–1976). The other members of the Gang of Four were Wang Hongwen, former textile mill worker who became Vice-Chairman of the CCP in 1973; Yao Wenyuan, editor at the *Shanghai Liberation Daily*, who became a Politburo member in 1973; and Zhang Qunqiao, secretary of CCP Shanghai Municipal Committee who became a Politburo member in 1973, then Vice Premier of the State Council in 1975.

[3] "The Cultural Revolution as Legacy and Precedent," Zenobia Lai, Elisabeth Wickerim, and Carol Wang, drafters, and Nathan Gin, Yuki Tsui, and Seren Tang, researchers, an HRIC Brief, *Advancing Social Justice, China Rights Forum* no. 4 (2005): 39; *http://www.hrichina.org/public/PDFs/ CRF.4.2005/CRF-2005-4_Revolution.pdf* (accessed June 9, 2009).

[4] "Memorial for Victims of the Chinese Cultural Revolution," Chinese Holocaust Memorial website, *http://www.chinese-memorial.org/* (accessed June 9, 2009); Stacey Mosher, "The Past is not Another Country: An Interview with Wang Youqin," *http://humanities.uchicago.edu/faculty/ywang/history/CRF-2005-4_Past.htm* (accessed June 9, 2009).

[5] Sources: "The Cultural Revolution as Legacy and Precedent," 37–39, and Jeffrey Hays, "Cultural Revolution—The End," Facts and Details website, *http://factsanddetails.com/china.php?itemid=66&catid=2&subcatid=6* (accessed June 9, 2009), and Feng Jicai, *Voices from the Whirlwind: An Oral History of the Chinese Cultural Revolution* (Pantheon, 1990), and Gao Yuan, *Born Red: A Chronicle of the Cultural Revolution* (Stanford University Press, 1987).

---

6 Andreas Lorenz, "The Chinese Cultural Revolution: Remembering Mao's Victims," trans. Christopher Sultan, *Spiegel Online International,* May 15, 2007; *http://www.spiegel.de/international/world/0,1518,483023,00.html* (accessed June 9, 2009).

7 See Michael Schoenhals's review of *Jiyi* ("Remembrance"), ed. Wu Di (Beijing) and He Shu (Chongqing); bi-weekly non-commercial electronic publication (distributed via the Internet to Cultural Revolution historians worldwide) in *The China Quarterly*, Volume 197, March 2009, 204–206.

8 "Examination 1977," All-China Women's Federation website, *http://www.womenofchina.cn/ Lifestyle/Leisure_Time/movie/210262.jsp* (accessed June 9, 2009).

DOCUMENT 19

The legacy of the Cultural Revolution, selected quotations

Quotation #1: Excerpt from the "Resolution on Certain Questions in the History of Our Party Since the Founding of the People's Republic of China," adopted by the Communist Party of China on June 27, 1981

Comrade Mao Zedong was a . . . great proletarian revolutionary . . . It is true that he made gross mistakes during the "cultural revolution," but, if we judge his activities as a whole, his contributions to the Chinese revolution far outweigh his mistakes.[1]

Quotation #2: Liu Xiaobo, a journalist and literary critic who has spent a total of four and half years in prison since taking part in the 1989 pro-democracy protests in China

*It can even be said that 30 years after the Cultural Revolution has ended, the national self-examination about this "catastrophe" has still not yet begun today. . . . The officials do not permit open discussion, the victims do not want to remember, and the persecutors are not willing to **repent**.*[2]

Quotation #3: Victim of the Cultural Revolution (anonymous)

Don't tell me that it was all the fault of the Gang of Four. If it was just the Gang of Four without the crowds, they could not have caused such massive evil.[3]

Quotation #4: A survivor of the Cultural Revolution

This generation is a special generation. We have a mission in our lives to fulfill our own values and also to do something to contribute to society.[4]

Quotation #5: Lui Binyan, a Chinese journalist

*Most Chinese would probably agree that the reforms that began in 1979 under Deng Xiaoping would never have taken place without [the Cultural Revolution] . . . The Red Guards who had followed Mao so **fanatically** grew **disillusioned**. They became the first generation capable of independent thinking, full of **insubordinate** spirit. It is this generation that forms the backbone of Chinese society. Many have become influential writers, scholars, journalists, and entrepreneurs, as well as middle- to high-ranking officials in the government, the army, and the Communist Party.*[5]

Quotation #6: Wu Shanren, former Red Guard

I think the Cultural Revolution was the happiest period of my life. There was something special about that time: the loyalty, the sense of solidarity, the confidence and the certainty.[6]

Quotation #7: Yang Yinzi, former Red Guard

It's strange I miss the past so much. I view the time I spent during the Cultural Revolution as my golden period. . . . On a superficial level things are much better. I've got more possessions. Books are widely available. But I no longer feel that there's any substance or intensity to my existence.[7]

Quotation #8: Chou Linlin, former Red Guard

My daughter knows nothing about the Cultural Revolution. She asks me lots of questions. . . . It's very difficult for me to share my history with her. It's hard for her to understand. What's the point of bothering her about stories of the past?[8]

Quotation #9: Song Xu, former Red Guard

*Many people now like to claim that, during the Cultural Revolution, we were victims of **indoctrination**. Well, if we were "victims" it was our choice. . . . I became a Red Guard out of self-interest. I wanted to belong and I was personally ambitious. What I did then is not so different from what I'm doing now. Money's the sign of prestige and success today, so money's the new idol in society. During the Cultural Revolution, politics was the measure of success, so Mao was the idol. . . . You want to make a comparison between my generation and the generation that followed? The members of my generation do still have an interest in larger political issues and do still care about society as a whole.[9]*

Quotation #10: Wang Xiaoying, former Red Guard

During the Cultural Revolution, nearly all of the nation's youth willingly joined Red Guard Organizations. We wanted to serve. The future we hoped to build never came, but this doesn't mean that all our sacrifices were meaningless and now are best forgotten. Our generation represents the tragic spirit of an era. . . . A few weeks ago, I was talking to my mother about the past. I asked her whether she believed she was a victim of the Cultural Revolution. She thought for a moment. "In one way or another," she replied, "everyone was a victim." She was right. When a whole nation goes through a dark period no one is spared.[10]

Quotation #11: Former Red Guard (anonymous)

*When I talk about the Cultural Revolution, I don't feel any **remorse**. I can confess what we did, but no regrets. When we joined the movement, we had no ulterior motives. We were dedicated and we suffered for it too. . . . It's not fair to put all the blame for what happened on us Red Guards. The Cultural Revolution was simply a policy misdirection. . . . You can't blame the Red Army soldiers, can you? Were their deaths worthless? In a war, when the commander makes mistakes, the common soldiers are still **martyrs**. Aren't they?*[11]

GLOSSARY

disillusioned: disappointed

fanatically: enthusiastically

indoctrination: brainwashing

insubordinate: rebellious

martyrs: people willing to die for their beliefs or cause

remorse: guilt, or sense of regret

repent: apologize

---

[1] "Peace, Development, Progress," International Department Central Committee of CPC website, www.idcpc.org.cn (accessed on June 9, 2009).

[2] DPA, "Beijing plays down 10 lost, chaotic years," Taipei Times, May 16, 2006; *http://www.taipeitimes.com/News/world/archives/2006/05/16/2003308448 (accessed June 9, 2009).*

[3] "The Cultural Revolution as Legacy and Precedent," Zenobia Lai, Elisabeth Wickerim, an HRIC Brief, Advancing Social Justice, China Rights Forum no. 4 (2005): 39; *http://www.hrichina.org/public/PDFs/ CRF.4.2005/CRF-2005-4_Revolution.pdf* (accessed June 9, 2009).

[4] Jeffrey Hays, "Cultural Revolution—The End," Facts and Details website, *http://factsanddetails.com/china.php?itemid =66&catid=2&subcatid=6* (accessed June 9, 2009).

[5] Ibid.

[6] Ashley, *Mao's Children in the New China: Voices From the Red Guard Generation*, 25.

[7] Ibid., 52.

[8] Ibid.,74.

[9] Ibid., 165–166.

[10] Ibid., 171.

[11] Feng, Op. Cit., 91.

☑ TEACHING STRATEGIES

☑ TEACHING STRATEGY: COMPREHENSION QUESTIONS

The discussion questions and activities suggested in this study guide require students to interpret, synthesize, and apply ideas from *Red Scarf Girl* in order to better understand history and human behavior. Students will feel more comfortable and successful addressing these complex questions if they first possess a basic understanding of events described in *Red Scarf Girl*. Teachers often use comprehension questions to assess the extent to which students are following the plot. Students' responses to comprehension questions can reveal areas of confusion that should be clarified before moving on to topics of greater complexity. We strongly suggest that comprehension questions are used only as a first step in students' exploration of *Red Scarf Girl*. Since the purpose of reading this text is to deepen students' historical understanding, ethical awareness, and critical thinking, it is crucial that students also have the opportunity to pursue questions requiring higher-order thinking skills.

Here are some ways the questions could be integrated into a lesson:

- As part of a written quiz
- Informally asking these questions during class
- As a "do now" or opener activity
- Assigning questions to students to answer and share with the class
- As a homework assignment

Prologue (p. 1)

1. Why did Ji-li's parents choose the name "Ji-li"? What does it mean?

2. Why did Ji-li wear a red scarf?

Chapter 1: "The Liberation Army Dancer" (pp. 3–18)

1. Why does the Liberation Army soldier visit Ji-li's school?

2. What do you think Ji-li's father means when he tells his daughter that she cannot audition for the Central Liberation Army Arts Academy because of "political considerations" and the "family's background"? Do you think Ji-li understands what her father means? What gives you this impression?

3. What was Ji-li's reaction to not being allowed to attend the audition?

4. Ji-li describes her family as "lucky" and "special." What evidence does she provide to support her view of her family as privileged?

5. List at least five reasons why Ji-li describes her life as "nearly perfect."

Chapter 2: "Destroy the Four Olds!" (pp. 19–37)

1. Ji-li often refers to how life was different in the past. List at least two examples of how life "used to be" in Shanghai, according to Ji-li.

2. What were the "Four Olds"? Why did Chairman Mao want the Four Olds to be destroyed? What examples does Ji-li give of destroying the Four Olds?

3. Humiliation is a theme in this memoir. Find an example of a moment when someone was being humiliated. Who was being humiliated? By whom? For what reason?

Chapter 3: "Writing *Da–zi–bao*" (pp. 38–51)

1. What is a *da-zi-bao*? What conflict did Ji-li confront when she was asked to write a *da-zi-bao*? What did she do?

2. On page 36, Ji-li remarks, "The world had turned upside down." What had happened to make Ji-li feel this way?

3. What happens to Ji-li's Aunt Xi-wen? How does Ji-li react to this treatment of her aunt? How do you think she feels about her behavior?

4. What is written about Ji-li on the *da-zi-bao*?

Chapter 4: "The Red Successors" (pp. 52–71)

1. What words and labels are used to describe someone who is an enemy of the revolution?

2. What is a Red Guard? What is a Red Successor? Why is Ji-li excluded from being a Red Successor?

3. What do you think "class status" means in China at this time? What types of people have a desirable class status? What types of people have an undesirable class status?

4. Why do Ji-li's classmates think she needs to remold herself?

Chapter 5: "Graduation" (pp. 72–79)

1. How were school assignments made before the Cultural Revolution? How are they being made now? What does Ji-li think of the new school assignment system?

2. Why is Ji-li so excited when she hears where she will be going to junior high school? What changes at the end of the chapter?

3. What does Ji-li think will happen to many of the books in the school library?

Chapter 6: "The Sound of Drums and Gongs" (pp. 80–99)

1. What were the Red Guards trying to find when they searched through houses?

2. What does "the sound of drums and gongs" represent?

3. Why do Ji-li's parents fire Song Po-po? How does Ji-li's role in her family change as a result?

4. Why does the Jiang family turn silk dresses into mops and paint red leather trunks black?

Chapter 7: "The Propaganda Wall" (pp. 100–117)

1. What was the propaganda wall?

2. What are the Five Black Categories?

3. What is the Precious Red Book?

4. What tasks did the Neighborhood Dictatorship Groups perform?

5. Who is Jia Hong-yu, and what does she tell Ji-li and her peers who had gathered in the cafeteria?

Chapter 8: "A Search in Passing" (pp. 118–139)

1. Why were Ji-li's parents burning photographs in their bathroom?

2. On page 126, Ji-li shares, "In the three months since the Cultural Revolution had started, changes had been so constant that I often felt lost." Identify at least three changes that Ji-li has experienced since the start of the Cultural Revolution.

3. What personal possession of Ji-li's is taken when the Red Guards search the family's house? Why is it confiscated?

4. What is the difference between how Ji-yong and Ji-li respond when special items are taken from them?

Chapter 9: "Fate" (pp. 140–155)

1. How does Shan-shan act toward his mother? Why do you think he acts this way?

2. What are some ways that Red Guards scared and humiliated people suspected of rightist or anti-revolutionary leanings?

3. What happened to Sang Hong-zhen, Du Hai's mother?

4. Why does Ji-li hate her grandfather?

Chapter 10: "Junior High School at Last" (pp. 156–172)

1. Describe Ji-li's first day of school. What disappointed her? What part of Ji-li's first day at junior high school in her new classroom does she enjoy the most?

2. Ji-li's father is forced to attend a political study class. What was the purpose of political study classes for adults like Ji-li's father?

3. How does Sun Lin-lin "rescue" Ji-li?

4. How does Ji-li react to being asked to join the propaganda group?

Chapter 11: "Locked Up" (pp. 173–190)

1. What was New Year's Day like before the Cultural Revolution, according to Ji-li? What is it like now?

2. Who is Uncle Fan and why was he crying?

3. Give an example of the Communist Party's "policy of psychological pressure."

4. A dilemma is when someone has to make a choice between two or more important values. What dilemmas do Ji-li and members of her family confront in this section? What values are at odds?

Chapter 12: "An Educable Child" (pp. 191–205)

1. Why does Ji-li decide to join the group preparing the Class Education Exhibition, despite her family background?

2. What is the Class Education Exhibition? What type of projects do the children work on?

3. Ji-li tells her friend Lin-lin about how Ji-li's father has been detained. How does Lin-lin respond?

4. On page 205, Chang Hong tells Ji-li, "But we can't allow personal matters to interfere with revolutionary duties." What do you think she means by this? What "personal matter" is she referring to?

Chapter 13: "Half–City Jiangs" (pp. 206–217)

1. Describe the policy of confession promoted by the Red Guards and those in charge of the Cultural Revolution. Who is asked to confess? About what crimes are they confessing? What is done to encourage people to confess?

2. What happens to Ji-li's father after the truth of Uncle Zhu's confession is revealed?

3. What does the *Workers' Revolt* newspaper say about the Jiang family? Is this information true or false?

4. At the beginning of this chapter, why does Ji-li want to change her name? What makes her change her mind?

Chapter 14: "The Class Education Exhibition" (pp. 218–229)

1. What story does Ji-li tell as part of the exhibition rehearsal?

2. After Ji-li receives praise for her role in the Class Education Exhibition, why is she replaced by Fang Fang?

3. On page 227, Ji-li says, "I felt like a small animal that had fallen into a trap, alone and helpless, and sure that the hunter was coming." What do you think Ji-li means when she says this? What is the trap she refers to in this statement? Who is the hunter?

4. What are the two choices Ji-li is given in her teacher's office by Thin-Face?

Chapter 15: "The Rice Harvest" (pp. 230–243)

1. Why is it so important for Ji-li's political life that she work in the countryside for her summer labor as opposed to a factory?

2. What kind of work does Ji-li perform in the countryside?

3. When Bai Shan offers to help Ji-li, how does she respond? Why do you think she responds this way?

4. What dream does Ji-li have in this chapter? What do you think it means?

Chapter 16: "The Incriminating Letter" (pp. 244–259)

1. What does the letter say that Ji-li finds on her mother's bed? Why would this letter get the family in trouble?

2. Where does Ji-li hide the letter?

3. What does Thin-Face do to try to get Ji-li to confess about the letter?

4. What are the consequences for Mom and Grandma for being labeled landlords' wives?

Chapter 17: "Sweeping" (pp. 260–264)

1. How has Ji-li's house changed since the beginning of *Red Scarf Girl*?

2. What type of work does Ji-li's grandmother have to do now that she has been classified as a landlord's wife?

3. Ji-li describes many worries in this chapter. What are a few of the things that she worries about?

4. At the end of this chapter, Ji-li describes how she has changed over the past two years since the start of the Cultural Revolution. What are some of the changes she names?

Epilogue (pp. 265–272)

1. How does Ji-li Jiang explain why so many people went along with the Cultural Revolution?

2. What important lesson does Ji-li take away from her experience growing up during the Cultural Revolution?

3. What happens to Ji-li's family after the Cultural Revolution?

4. Why does Ji-li decide to move to the United States?

5. According to Ji-li, what happened to people who committed crimes during the Cultural Revolution?

6. In the final line of the epilogue, Ji-li writes, "I hope this book will be part of that mission." What is the mission she refers to in this quotation?

☑ TEACHING STRATEGY: FOUND POEMS

Found poems are created through the careful selection and organization of words and phrases from existing text. Writing found poems provides a structured way for students to review material and synthesize their learning.

INSTRUCTIONS FOR CREATING A FOUND POEM

Step one: Creating a list of words, phrases, and quotations

Review any text related to your study of *Red Scarf Girl* and the Cultural Revolution, including work on the walls of your classroom, journal entries, primary source documents, and the book itself. As you look over these texts, record words, phrases, or quotations that are particularly interesting or meaningful to you. Try to identify at least 20 different words or phrases so that you have plenty of ideas from which to choose when writing your poem.

Step two: Determining a theme and message

Look over your list. Try to identify a theme and message that represents the language you have selected. A theme is a broad concept such as *obedience* or *loyalty*. A message is a specific idea you would like to express about this theme. For example, looking over the language you have selected, you might realize that *propaganda* is a theme that emerges. "Read, watch, listen, and THINK" is an example of a message that relates to this theme. Often it is helpful to do this step with a partner. Trade lists. Then describe the themes or main ideas you see in your partner's list.

Step three: Selecting additional language

When writing a found poem, you can only use words that you have collected from other sources. So, once you select a theme and a message, you may need to review your materials again to collect additional language for your found poem.

Step four: Composing your poem

Now arrange the language you have selected. One approach is to write all of the words and phrases on slips of paper, so you can move them around until you find a composition that pleases you. While you cannot add your own words when creating a found poem (not even articles or prepositions), you can repeat words or phrases as often as you like. Also, when composing your poem, you do not need to use all of the words or phrases you selected.

☑ TEACHING STRATEGY: JIGSAW

Using the jigsaw teaching strategy is one way to help students understand and retain information. This strategy asks a group of students to become "experts" on a specific text or body of knowledge and then share that material with another group of students. These "teaching groups" contain one student from each of the "expert" groups. Students often feel more accountable for learning material when they know they are responsible for teaching the content to their peers. The jigsaw strategy is most effective when students know that they will be using all of the information they have learned from each other to create a final product, participate in a class discussion, or acquire material that will be on a test.

Step one: Preparation

Select the material you want students to explore. It might be a collection of documents (e.g., readings, images, charts), or it could be a series of questions. Also, decide how many students you would like to work together in an "expert" group. Teachers often find that groups of three to five students work best. Sometimes it makes sense to form groups randomly (e.g., by counting off), while other times you might want to divide the class in advance to balance strengths, needs, and interests. You can assign the same material to more than one group. *Example: Use documents 7–11 to help students explore the role of Red Guards during the Cultural Revolution.*

Step two: Students work in expert groups

Distribute the materials to small groups of students who are responsible for reviewing this material so that they can share it with others as "experts." Expert groups work best when students have clear expectations about the type of information they are supposed to share with their peers. Therefore, it is often helpful to provide a chart or a series of questions that students answer together in their expert groups. Because students typically move to their teaching group individually, it is important that all group members understand the material they are responsible for presenting. To avoid having students present inaccurate or misleading information, it is important for teachers to review and approve of the content the expert group members plan to share. *Example: Ask expert groups to answer the question, "What information does this document reveal about Red Guards?" You might require groups to come up with a list of five to ten things they learn about Red Guards from that document.*

Step three: Students meet in teaching groups

After the expert groups have a solid understanding of the material they will be presenting, you can assign students to teaching groups. Teaching groups are typically composed of one member from each expert group, or one student representing each of the materials being studied in this lesson. Experts take turns presenting information. Often teachers ask students to take notes while the experts present. *Example: As each expert presents, students add to their lists of information about Red Guards.*

Step four: Synthesis and reflection

Teaching groups can be assigned a task that requires them to synthesize the information that has been shared, such as answering a larger question, comparing texts, or generating a plan of action. Students can synthesize information individually or in pairs. It is appropriate to structure a class discussion that asks students to draw from the material they just learned to answer a question about history and apply this information to society today. *Example: Based on the information from* Red Scarf Girl *and the documents they just shared with each other, small groups or individual students can create a list called "Top Ten Ways Chinese Youth Were Told to Think and Act During the Cultural Revolution." This can lead to a class discussion comparing the messages transmitted to Chinese youth during the Cultural Revolution to the messages disseminated to youth today.*

☑ TEACHING STRATEGY: WORD WALL

A "word wall" is a large display in the classroom where the meanings of important ideas are displayed using words and pictures. Because the vocabulary used in *Red Scarf Girl* may be unfamiliar to students, creating a word wall is one way to help them comprehend and interpret the text.

Step one: Preparation

Select a place in the room for your word wall. Large sheets of poster paper or a dedicated whiteboard work well.

Step two: Building your word wall

Suggested words for your word wall include: Communist Party, Communism, People's Liberation Army, political background, class status, bourgeoisie, capitalist/capitalism, revolutionary, counterrevolutionary, Chairman Mao Zedong, conservative, revolution, Cultural Revolution, proletarian, reactionary, revisionist, rightist, socialism. Before you begin reading *Red Scarf Girl*, you might assign students, possibly working in pairs, a term to define for the class word wall. You can also require students to present an image or graphic that will help students remember the meaning of this word.

Step three: Adding to your word wall

New terms can be added to the word wall as needed. Students can also update the definitions on their word wall as they develop a deeper understanding of key terms.

☑ TEACHING STRATEGY: ANTICIPATION GUIDES

Anticipation guides ask students to form an opinion about key themes and ideas that will emerge in a text they are about to read. Completing anticipation guides prepares students to recognize and connect to these themes as they surface in their reading.

Step one: Selecting statements for the anticipation guide

The most effective statements relate to universal themes and dilemmas that will emerge in a text and are phrased in ways that make sense when applied to events in the text, and to situations in students' lives. Below are suggested statements you could use when creating an anticipation guide to prepare students to read *Red Scarf Girl*:

- It is possible to build a society where everyone is equal.
- Under most circumstances, people will go along with the crowd.
- People should be loyal to their country and follow the laws set by the leaders of government.
- After a community has been through a time of conflict or violence, it is better for everyone to move on and forget the crimes or hardships of the past.
- It is never appropriate to exclude someone from membership in a group.
- Individuals should not be held responsible for decisions made by their relatives and ancestors.
- Books or other media that promote ideas harmful to society should be banned and/or destroyed.
- Education is a powerful weapon that shapes how young people think and act as community members.

Step two: Deciding how you want students to respond to these statements

Often teachers prepare a worksheet or graphic organizer that structures students' responses by asking them to decide if they strongly agree, agree, disagree, or strongly disagree with the statement and then explain why. Sometimes students are asked to provide a response in the form of a numerical ranking. For example, 1 can represent the strongest agreement, and 10 can represent the strongest disagreement. It is also possible to give students one or more statements to respond to in their journals.

Step three: Reflecting on statements again after completing the text

Often teachers have students review their anticipation guides after completing a text, noting how their experience with new material might have changed their thinking. Reflections can be presented in writing and/or through discussion. Often the statements used in anticipation guides make effective jumping-off points for essay writing.

☑ TEACHING STRATEGY: HUMAN TIMELINE

The human timeline teaching strategy uses movement to help students understand and remember the chronology of events.

Step one: Pre-class setup

The timelines found on pages 140–143 of this study guide can be used as the text for this activity. By combining, deleting, or adding events, you can adapt this timeline to best meet the needs of your students. Some teachers assign each student his or her own timeline item to present, and other teachers have found that this activity works best if timeline items are presented by pairs. In preparation for this activity, we suggest placing each of the events on an index card or a standard-size sheet of paper, along with the date when it occurred. Rather than distributing the timeline slips randomly, you might want to give certain students easier or more challenging items, depending on their strengths and weaknesses.

Next, because students are able to see and hear each other better in a *U*-shaped line than in a straight-line formation, identify a location in or near your classroom that will allow for students to form a *U*-shape. Students stand for this activity, or chairs can be arranged in a *U*-shape.

Step two: Individual or pairs prepare timeline presentations

Whether students work individually or in pairs, here is an example of instructions you can provide:

1. Read over your timeline event once or twice.
2. Rewrite the timeline item in your own words. Do not read from your timeline slip when you present this event to the class; rather, explain this event in your own words. If you are having trouble writing the statement in your own words, ask for help.
3. An extension of this activity asks students to create or find an image that corresponds to their event.

Step three: Building your human timeline

Invite students to line up in the order of their events. Then have students present their events. After an event is presented, students can suggest possible causes of the event and pose questions. These questions can be posted on the board for students to answer later.

Step four (optional): Retaining information

After all students have presented their events, sometimes teachers give students a timeline with relevant dates but no descriptions. Based on what they recall from the human timeline activity, students complete this timeline. This can be done individually or in small groups. Sometimes teachers ask students to add images to their timelines. Students can also add events from *Red Scarf Girl* to their timelines.

☑ TEACHING STRATEGY: IDENTITY CHARTS

Identity charts are a graphic tool that helps students consider the many factors that shape who we are as individuals and as communities. They can be used to deepen students' understanding of themselves, historical and literary figures, groups, and nations.

Step one: Preparation

Before creating identity charts, you might have the class brainstorm categories we consider when thinking about the question, "Who am I?" These might include our role in a family (e.g., daughter, sister, mother, etc.), our hobbies and interests (e.g., guitar player, being a football fan, etc.), our background (e.g., religion, race, nationality, hometown, or place of birth), and our physical characteristics. It is often helpful to show students a completed identity chart before they create one of their own. Alternatively, you could begin this activity by having students create identity charts for themselves. After sharing their charts, students can create a list of the categories they have used to describe themselves.

Step two: Creating identity charts for Ji–li Jiang

First, ask students to write Ji-li's name in the center of a piece of paper. Then students can look through *Red Scarf Girl* for evidence that helps them answer the question, "Who is Ji-li?" Encourage students to include quotations from the text on their identity charts, as well as their own interpretations of Ji-li based on their reading. Students can complete identity charts individually or in small groups. Alternatively, students could contribute ideas to a class version of an identity chart for Ji-li that you keep on the classroom wall.

Step three: Using identity charts to track how Ji–li changes throughout this memoir

Reviewing and revising this identity chart after each reading assignment is one way to help students keep track of how Ji-li changes throughout the novel. Alternatively, you might have students create a new identity chart for Ji-li at the end of the memoir. By comparing this identity chart to the one that they made for Ji-li at the beginning of the book, students can trace the development of this character. This exercise provides evidence that can inform a conversation about the various factors that contributed to these changes.

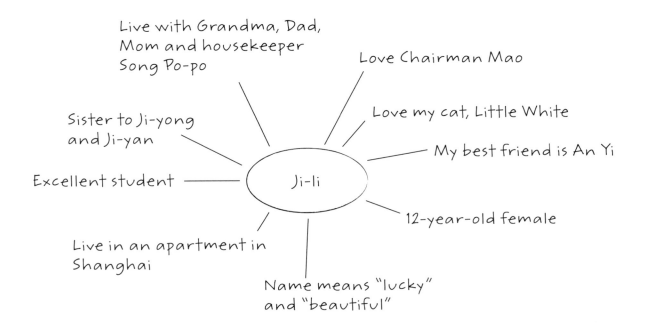

Live with Grandma, Dad, Mom and housekeeper Song Po-po

Love Chairman Mao

Sister to Ji-yong and Ji-yan

Love my cat, Little White

Excellent student

My best friend is An Yi

Ji-li

12-year-old female

Live in an apartment in Shanghai

Name means "lucky" and "beautiful"

☑ TEACHING STRATEGY: READER'S THEATER

Reader's theater is an effective way to help students process dilemmas that characters experience throughout this memoir. In this activity, groups of students are assigned a small portion of the text to present to their peers. Unlike the presentation of plot skits, reader's theater asks students to create a performance that reveals a message, theme, or conflict represented by the text. The more experience students have with reader's theater, the more proficient they become at using the words of the text to depict concepts and ideas.

Step one: Preparation

Depending on how many students are in your class, you will likely need to identify four to five excerpts or "scenes" for this activity. Typically, groups of four to six students are assigned different sections of a text to interpret, although it is certainly possible to have groups interpret the same excerpt. When selecting excerpts for use with reader's theater, keep in mind these suggestions:

- Shorter excerpts allow students to look more deeply at specific language than do longer excerpts. Often excerpts are only a few paragraphs long.
- Use excerpts that contain one main action or decision-making point.
- Excerpts should address an important theme in the text; they should represent more than just the plot line.

Example: The chapter "Writing Da-zi-bao*" provides several moments that are appropriate for reader's theater. For instance, groups could be assigned the following moments to present: 1) when Ji-li can't decide what to write on her* da-zi-bao *(pp. 38–39); 2) when Ji-li reads Yin Lan-lan's* da-zi-bao *(p. 40 to middle of p. 42); 3) when Ji-li decides to write her* da-zi-bao *(pp. 42–43); 4) when Ji-li joins the group to denounce her aunt (pp. 44–45); 5) when Du-Hai denounces Aunt Xi-wen (pp. 46–47); and 6) when a* da-zi-bao *is written about Ji-li (pp. 48–51).*

Step two: Reading selections

Before groups are assigned scenes to interpret, give students the opportunity to read the selections silently and aloud. This step familiarizes students with the language of the text. After the text is read aloud, invite students to ask clarifying questions about the vocabulary or plot. That way, students can begin their group work ready to interpret their assigned scenes.

Step three: Groups prepare performances

1. Assign scenes (excerpts) to groups.

2. In their small groups, students read their assigned scenes aloud again. As they read, students should pay attention to theme, language, and tone. You might ask students to highlight or underline the words that stand out to them. Groups may choose to read their scenes two or three times and then have a conversation about the words and phrases they have highlighted.

3. Then groups discuss the scene. At the end of this discussion, students should agree on the words, theme, or message represented in this excerpt that they would most like to share with the class. To help structure the groups' conversations, you might provide them with a series of questions to answer. *Example: What conflict is expressed in this excerpt? What theme is represented? What words or phrases are most important? What is the message of this text? What is most important or interesting about the words or ideas in this excerpt?*

4. Now students are ready to prepare their performances. Students should be reminded that the goal is not to perform a skit of the scene, but to use specific language (words and phrases) to represent the conflict, theme, and/or underlying message of that excerpt. Performances can be silent, or students can use voice in creative ways, such as by composing a choral reading that emphasizes key phrases. Students can use movement, or they can hold their body positions to create an image frozen in time, much like a photograph. It often helps to give students a list of guidelines or suggestions to follow when preparing their presentations. *Examples:*

   • *Repeat key words, phrases, or sentences.*

   • *Read some or all of your selection as a group, as part of a group, or as individuals.*

   • *Alter the order of the text.*

   • *Position yourselves around the room as you see fit.*

   • *You may not use props, but you can use body positioning to achieve a certain effect.*

   • *Everyone has to participate.*

Step four: Performances

There are many ways to structure performances. Some teachers ask students to take notes while all groups perform. Then students use their notes to guide their reactions to the performances. Alternatively, teachers ask students to comment immediately after each performance. It is best if students' comments are phrased in the form of positive feedback rather than in the form of a critique (e.g., "It would have been better if . . .") Before debriefing performances, you can go over the types of comments that are appropriate and inappropriate, or you can provide students with sentence starters they could use when phrasing their feedback.

Examples of starters that frame positive feedback:

- *It was powerful for me when . . .*
- *The performance that helped me understand* Red Scarf Girl *in a new way was . . . because . . .*
- *It was interesting how . . .*
- *One performance that stood out to me was . . . because . . .*
- *I was surprised when . . . because . . .*

☑ TEACHING STRATEGY: CHARACTER CHARTS

Graphic organizers, like the sample below, can be used to help students organize information about major and minor characters in a text. Some teachers assign students specific characters to "follow" and then meet in groups to complete the whole chart.

Character's Name	Biographical information	Major actions taken by this character (with page numbers)	Important quotations said by this character (with page numbers)
Ji-li Jiang			
Xi-reng Jiang			
Chen Ying			
Grandma Cao			
Ji-yong			
Ji-yun			
Song Po-po			
An Yi			
Du Hai			
Yin Lan-lan			
Sun Lin-lin			
Chang Hong			
Bai Shan			
Aunt Jiang Xi-wen			
"Six-Fingers" Mr. Ni			
Uncle Zhu			
Uncle Tian			
Uncle Fan			

☑ TEACHING STRATEGY: DEVELOPING MEDIA LITERACY: ANALYZING PROPAGANDA AND OTHER IMAGES

The following Describe-Identify-Interpret-Evaluate process can be used to guide students' analysis of propaganda posters or other images:

1. **Describe** what you see in as much detail as possible. List information about recognizable images, colors, and composition (placement of objects on the page).
2. **Identify** basic information about this poster. Who made it? When? Who was the intended audience?
3. **Interpret** the message expressed by this image. What do you think it means? What gives you this idea? What techniques were used to help express this message?
4. **Evaluate** the possible impact of this poster. How might the message expressed in this poster have influenced the ideas and actions of people living in China? What does this poster tell you about life in China during the Cultural Revolution?

The next page includes a sample graphic organizer students can use to record information about the propaganda posters they are analyzing.

GRAPHIC ORGANIZER: ANALYZING CHINESE PROPAGANDA POSTERS

Describe what you see in as much detail as possible. List information about recognizable images, colors, and composition (placement of objects on the page).	
Identify basic information about this poster. Who made it? When? Who was the intended audience?	
Interpret the message expressed by this image. What do you think it means? What gives you this idea? What techniques were used to help express this message?	
Evaluate the possible impact of this poster. How might the message expressed in this poster have influenced the ideas and actions of people living in China? What does this poster tell you about life in China during the Cultural Revolution?	

☑ TEACHING STRATEGY: TEXT-TO-SELF, TEXT-TO-TEXT, TEXT-TO-WORLD

This teaching strategy deepens students' understanding of a text. It is best used after students have sufficient comprehension of the material.

Step one: Text-to-self

Ask students to answer questions about the reading that relate to themselves.

Examples:

- *What I just read reminds me of the time when I was included or excluded . . .*
- *I agree with/understand what I just read because in my own life . . .*
- *I don't agree with what I just read because in my own life . . .*

Step two: Text-to-text

Ask students to answer questions about how the text reminds them of another piece of text.

Examples:

- *What I just read reminds me of another story/book I read/song I heard/ movie I saw because . . .*
- *What I just read reminds me of the ostracism case study we read in lesson two because . . .*

Step three: Text-to-world

Ask students to answer questions about how the text relates to the larger world.

Examples:

- *What I just read reminds me of this thing that happened in history because . . .*
- *What I just read reminds me of what's going on in my community/country/ in the world now because . . .*

☑ TEACHING STRATEGY: FOUR-CORNERS DEBATE

A four-corners debate requires students to show their position on a specific statement (strongly agree, agree, disagree, strongly disagree) by standing in a particular corner of the room. This activity elicits the participation of all students by requiring everyone to take a position.

Step one: Preparation

Label the four corners of the room with signs reading "strongly agree," "agree," "disagree," "strongly disagree." Generate a list of controversial statements related to the material being studied. Statements most likely to encourage discussion typically do not have one correct or obvious answer; elicit nuanced arguments (e.g., "This might be a good idea some of the time, but not all of the time") and represent respected values on both sides of the debate. *Examples: The statements on the anticipation guide could be used for a four-corners debate. Here are some additional statements that emphasize dilemmas raised in* Red Scarf Girl:

- *The needs of larger society are more important than the needs of the individual. (Or, in the words of Chang Hong, "We can't allow personal matters to interfere with revolutionary duties.")*
- *The purpose of schooling is to prepare youth to be good citizens.*
- *Individuals can choose their own destiny; their choices are not dictated or limited by the constraints of society.*
- *One should always resist unfair laws, regardless of the consequences.*
- *I am only responsible for myself.*

Step two: Introducing statements

Distribute statements and give students the opportunity to respond to them in writing. Many teachers provide students with a graphic organizer or worksheet that requires students to mark their opinion (strongly agree, agree, disagree, strongly disagree) and then provide a brief explanation.

Step three: Discussion

After students have considered their personal response to the statements, read one of the statements aloud, and ask students to move to the corner of the room that best represents their opinion. Once students are in their places, ask for volunteers to justify their position. When doing so, they should refer to evidence from history, especially from material they learned in this unit, as well as other relevant information from their own experiences. Encourage students to switch corners if someone presents an idea that causes a change of mind. After a representative from each corner has defended his or her position, you can allow students to question each other's evidence and ideas. This is an appropriate time to remind students about norms for having a respectful, open discussion of ideas.

Step four: Reflection

Ask students to reflect on how their ideas may have changed after participating in this activity. Some of their views may have been strengthened by the addition of new evidence and arguments, while others may have changed altogether. It is quite possible that some students will be more confused or uncertain about their views after the four-corners debate. While uncertainty can feel uncomfortable, it is an important part of the understanding process and represents the authentic wrestling with moral questions that have no clear right or wrong answers.

TIMELINE OF MODERN CHINA SINCE 1949

1949

Establishment of the People's Republic of China

With the support of a majority of Chinese citizens, Chairman Mao Zedong establishes a new Chinese government based on the principles of communism and led by the Chinese Communist Party (CCP). The CCP initiates land-distribution programs (giving peasants land previously owned by landlords) and builds new industries. Women are given equal rights in marriage and divorce.

1956–1957

The Hundred Flowers Movement and the Anti-Rightist Campaign

In order to improve the workings of the government, Mao invites the public to criticize government officials by issuing a call to "let a hundred flowers bloom, let a hundred schools of thought contend." The criticisms are much harsher than Mao expected and even attack his leadership. So he orders a harsh crackdown called the Anti-Rightist Campaign, in which hundreds of thousands of people, mostly intellectuals, are labeled "rightists," or enemies of the Communist Party, and many of them are sent to labor reform camps.

1958–1960

The Great Leap Forward

The "Great Leap Forward" is a program designed to rapidly modernize China's economy and create a more equal society. As part of this initiative, Mao orders rural Chinese to form communes (large groups of people working together) to farm the land and operate industry more efficiently. A combination of factors, including Mao's overzealous implementation of policies and bad weather, results in a massive famine, causing the deaths of an estimated 20 million Chinese children, women, and men.

1962–1965

Mao's doubts about China's future begin to grow

Chairman Mao grows increasingly unhappy about the direction China has gone in since the Great Leap Forward and concludes that it is in danger of returning to capitalism.

1966

The Cultural Revolution begins

Mao calls for a "Great Proletarian Cultural Revolution" to rid China of "revisionists," people suspected of bringing the country down the road to capitalism. Students in Chinese high schools and universities form organizations, called Red Guards, who swear loyalty to Chairman Mao. With Mao's blessing, the Red Guards carry out the Cultural Revolution's aim to destroy the "Four Olds"—old culture, old customs, old habits, and old ideas—while creating a society dedicated to the teachings of Chairman Mao.

1968

Red Guards are dismantled

After nearly two years of violence and chaos, including fierce fighting among Red Guard factions, Chairman Mao sends the army to dismantle the Red Guards and to bring order to the cities. Under the direction of the army, schools reopen. In December, Chairman Mao announces the "Up to the Mountains, Down to the Villages" campaign. As many as 16 million young people from the cities are sent to rural areas to perform manual labor and be "re-educated" by the peasants.

1968–1972

Political violence continues

In a series of political campaigns that involve restoring order and settling old scores from the first years of the Cultural Revolution, perhaps 1.5 to 2 million people are killed. In most cases, the army was actively involved in these campaigns or stood by while the violence occurred.

1973
U.S. President Richard Nixon visits China

When Chairman Mao greets United States President Richard Nixon in Beijing, it signals an end to Chinese isolation from the West.

1976
Chairman Mao dies, and the Cultural Revolution ends

In September, Chairman Mao dies, leaving Hua Guofeng as chairman of the Chinese Communist Party. In October, Hua arrests the "Gang of Four," which includes Mao's wife and three other radical leaders of the Cultural Revolution. Hua declares that the arrest of the Gang marks the formal end of the Cultural Revolution.

1977–1978
Deng Xiaoping emerges as China's most powerful leader

In order to help run the government, Hua Guofeng restores to office Deng Xiaoping, one of the top Communist Party leaders purged during the Cultural Revolution for being disloyal to Mao. Deng gradually establishes his position as China's most powerful leader. Under Deng, almost all of the policies established during the Cultural Revolution are reversed. For example, university entrance exams are re-established, and youth who had been sent to the countryside are permitted to return to the city. Over the next decade, China embarks on a program of bold economic reform and opening to the outside world.

1981
Chinese government officially calls the Cultural Revolution a mistake

In 1981, the Chinese Communist Party adopts a resolution that retroactively places the blame for the wrongdoings of the Cultural Revolution on Mao Zedong and the Gang of Four and rehabilitates many of Mao's political opponents who had been killed, jailed, or disgraced during the Cultural Revolution. The resolution concludes that, overall, Mao's achievements greatly outweighed his mistakes.

1989
Tiananmen Square democracy protests

While China's economy flourishes in the 1980s, some believe that political freedom suffers. In April, the death of Hu Yaobang, a Chinese official who advocated for greater democracy in China, motivates university students to demand democratic reforms, such as greater freedom of speech. Workers and intellectuals eventually join the hundreds of thousands of students who are protesting in Beijing's Tiananmen Square. On May 13, some of the protesters begin a hunger strike. On June 4, Deng Xiaoping, the leader of China's government, orders the army to enter the square to end the protests. Hundreds of Chinese protesters are killed by their own government. In defense of its actions, the Chinese government says it took the necessary actions to end a counterrevolutionary rebellion.

1989–present
Economic development and political repression

Deng Xiaoping dies in 1997, but his successors as China's top leaders, Jiang Zemin and Hu Jintao, carry out Deng's vision for China. During these years, China becomes a leading economy in the world while continuing to limit political freedom.

CULTURAL REVOLUTION TIMELINE 1966–1968

This timeline identifies major events that occur during the years covered by Ji–li Jiang in *Red Scarf Girl*.

May 16, 1966
"May 16 Circular" distributed by the Chinese Communist Party (CCP)

This official government statement says that Chinese culture must be cleansed of anti-Party, "black" elements. According to the "May 16 Circular," the CCP would be removing those with "bourgeois" tendencies who hold positions in the CCP, the government, the army, and other influential areas in society.

May 25, 1966
Da-zi-bao posted against professors

The first *da-zi-bao* (big character poster) is written against professors at Beijing University for being enemies of the Chinese Communist Party and for being against class struggle. As other students learn about this action, they began writing *da-zi-bao* against their professors.

May 29, 1966
Red Guards established

Students at an elite middle school establish the first group of Red Guards for the purpose of eliminating the enemies of Chairman Mao and those who oppose the ideals of the Chinese Communist Party.

August 5, 1966
Chairman Mao supports the Red Guards

In a *da-zi-bao*, Chairman Mao asks students to "Bombard the Headquarters" of the Chinese Communist Party. With Mao's support, Red Guards continue to post *da-zi-bao* criticizing teachers and Party officials.

August 8, 1966
The Cultural Revolution officially begins

In an official statement called the "Sixteen Points Directive," the Chinese Communist Party calls for a "Great Proletarian Cultural Revolution" to rid China of elements that are against Chairman Mao Zedong's thought and the ideals of class struggle. This document outlines a plan for how the Cultural Revolution should be conducted.

August 18, 1966
Red Guards rally in Beijing

An estimated 13 million Red Guards from around China travel to Beijing between August and November to show their support for the Cultural Revolution. At the first rally on August 18, 1966, Chairman Mao directs the large crowd to "destroy the Four Olds" (old culture, old customs, old habits, and old ideas—anything linked to China's "imperial" and "bourgeois" past).

September–December 1966
Red Guards take over

Schools are closed. Red Guards conduct house searches to "destroy the Four Olds." They hold large meetings where teachers, Party officials, professionals, and other "black elements" are humiliated, criticized, and sometimes physically beaten.

January 1967
Mao intensifies the Cultural Revolution

In an article published in the *People's Daily*, the main newspaper in China, Chairman Mao directs local leaders to criticize themselves as he praises the Red Guards. Local governments shut down as officials are denounced. With nobody in charge, Red Guard groups compete for power. Violence and chaos escalate.

Spring 1968
Propaganda campaign intensifies

Under the leadership of Jiang Qing, Chairman Mao's wife, a national program begins to promote Chairman Mao and his ideas. Millions of copies of Mao's selected quotations—*The Little Red Book*—are distributed. In study sessions for the young and old, Chinese are required to memorize Mao's teachings.

July 1968
The end of the Red Guards

Nearly two years of violence and chaos have harmed China's economy and resulted in the widespread loss of human lives and property. Chairman Mao sends the army to dismantle the Red Guards and bring order to the cities. Under the direction of the army, schools reopen. The Chinese government implements a program called "Up to the Mountains, Down to the Villages," which sends as many as 16 million former Red Guards from the cities to work alongside peasants in rural areas.

CREDITS

Document 17, Interview #1 contains excerpts from *Mao's Children in the New China*, by Yarong Jiang, copyright © 2000. Published by Routledge. Reproduced by permission of Taylor & Francis Books UK.

Document 17, Interview #3 is excerpted from *Voices from the Whirlwind* by Feng Jicai, copyright © 1991 by Random House, Inc. Copyright © 1990 by Foreign Languages Press. Used by permission of Pantheon Books, a division of Random House, Inc.